CATHEDRALS
IN BRITAIN & IRELAND

William Anderson · Clive Hicks

CATHEDRALS
IN BRITAIN & IRELAND
From early times to the reign of Henry VIII

Charles Scribner's Sons
NEW YORK

Copyright © 1978 William Anderson and Clive Hicks

First American edition published by Charles Scribner's
Sons, 1978

This book was designed and produced by
Blacker Calmann Cooper Ltd, London

Copyright under the Berne Convention

1 3 5 7 9 11 13 15 17 19 I/C 20 18 16 14 12 10 8 6 4 2

Printed in Great Britain

Library of Congress Catalog Card Number 77-92814
ISBN 0-684-15657-1

Contents

Preface

WE OFFER IN THIS BOOK a portrait gallery of most of those cathedrals built in the British Isles up to the period of the Reformation which survive in whole or in part. It is the first attempt to describe these cathedrals grouped on this wider geographical basis for over a century. The portraits are in pictures and words, often, for reasons of space, swift impressions and brief descriptions. Our survey covers all the English medieval cathedrals, as well as the major English abbey and collegiate churches which were made cathedrals at the Reformation or in the last and the present centuries. We describe the four Welsh cathedrals, nine of the fourteen Scottish medieval cathedrals together with St Giles, Edinburgh, made a cathedral in the seventeenth century, and nineteen cathedrals of the thirty-six Irish medieval dioceses. The medieval cathedrals which we have not illustrated and provided with individual descriptions are mentioned in the résumé on pages 175–176. Apart from monographs on single buildings, most recent treatments of the subject discuss the cathedrals according to period and style and concentrate largely on architectural features. Although this method is adopted briefly in the introduction, we have chosen to stress the individual qualities of each cathedral from the points of view of their history, their sites, their particular atmospheres and their furnishings, as well as their architectural qualities.

We must both acknowledge with gratitude the kindnesses we have received from the clergy and officers of many of the cathedrals we describe here, and we must thank them for the facilities they have provided for photography. We particularly appreciate the special facilities for access and photography provided at Lincoln, and the assistance of the chapter clerk. We also wish to acknowledge the permission granted by the Dean and chapter of Durham to take photographs. Our debt to some of the many writers on the subject is acknowledged in the short bibliography. Thanks are due to the Princeton University Press for allowing us to use the quotation from Abbot Suger on page 18 which is taken from pages 63 and 65 of *Abbot Suger on the Abbey Church of St Denis and its art treasures*, edited and translated by E. Panofsky (1946). We would also like to thank our friends at Blacker Calmann Cooper Ltd., John Calmann, Elwyn Blacker, Elisabeth Ingles, Sarah Riddell and Lavinia Keef for their help and encouragement during the writing and compilation of this book.

W.A.   C.H.

Introduction

Holy men and holy places

In AD 306 the Roman legions at York proclaimed Constantine their emperor, and so set off the train of events that led to Christianity becoming the state religion of the empire. York Minster, whose magnificent west front appears on the facing page, stands on part of the site of the Roman legionary fortress. From being a persecuted minority and then an embattled sect, Christians, no longer having to practise their rites in secret or in obscure buildings, could now proclaim the triumph of the faith in the grandeur of their constructions. From this followed the building of the great basilicas, most notably that of St Peter's at Rome in AD 325, from which the tradition of the cathedrals described in this book largely derives. The name cathedral describes a church in which the bishop of a diocese has his *cathedra* or throne. His diocese is also called a see and is named after the town or city in which he sits, although in Scotland the bishop sometimes took his title from a territory. In these early churches the throne was placed behind the altar in the apse in the manner still to be seen at Norwich and recently revived at Canterbury. Later it was moved to what is called the gospel side of the chancel (the right facing the high altar), as can be seen on pages 19 and 79. The throne symbolized the throne of God; the bishop sat on it as the heir by apostolic succession to St Peter, as the spiritual father of his people and as the sole guardian of certain powers entrusted to him alone.

The symbolic importance of the throne may be illustrated by one story. After St Augustine of Canterbury arrived in England to begin his mission in AD 597, he arranged a meeting with the bishops of the Welsh and of the other regions where the Celts had preserved Christianity throughout the invasions of the pagan Saxons. At that meeting he was under orders from Pope Gregory the Great to secure the submission of all the native bishops, but he interpreted those commands too rigidly and would not rise from his chair to greet them. Outraged by his discourtesy, they refused all his requests to bring their churches into common observance with Rome. They had much reason to feel affronted: well before Augustine's arrival, St Ninian at Whithorn in Galloway and St Columba at Iona (*pages* 134–135) had begun the conversion of Scotland while St Patrick had, in a spiritual sense, conquered Ireland. St Patrick said that those wretches who adore the sun must give way to the true sun, Christ. Celtic Christianity had its own indigenous strengths: its monastic forms in Ireland came originally from Syria and Egypt, then through Tours in France and had, therefore, bypassed the modifications and observances of Rome. In Ireland greater social and political importance was attached to the abbot than to the bishop who was generally one of the monks under the abbot's

YORK MINSTER: **the west front**

CANTERBURY: **the chair of St Augustine**

supervision carrying out episcopal functions. This helps to explain why so many of the earlier Irish cathedrals form part of groups of monastic buildings, as at Clonmacnois (*pages* 152–154), Kilmacduagh (*pages* 170–171) or Glendalough (*pages* 161–162).

Although the two sects of Christianity, the Roman and the Celtic, were not to settle their differences for many years, they agreed on one thing: the urgent necessity of converting the barbarous and pagan Saxon tribes. Travelling over the moss-grown Roman roads, Paulinus reached York and converted the great warrior, Edwin. Coming south from Iona, Aidan, 'the candle of the North', worked wonders and miracles in Northumbria. Soon from amongst those they converted there arose saints of Saxon birth of whom, perhaps, the most remarkable was St Cuthbert whose body now rests at Durham. After the martyrdom or natural death of these missionaries and saints, the presence of their bodies added the sanctity of their memories to the holiness of the shrines where they lay. When, with the revival of Roman skills and technology in the Romanesque style of the eleventh century, the first great cathedrals of the Norman period were erected, they frequently arose on sites long hallowed by generations of the pious and of pilgrims. Men and women of exceptional holiness were buried in places of honour, sometimes outside a church or in the porch and sometimes in the crypt. At Kildare in the seventh century the shrines of St Brigid and Bishop Conlaeth lay on either side of the high altar, surmounted by crowns of silver and gold. From early days it was believed that these saints could continue to work miracles and wonders, curing the sick and the lame, making the childless fertile, sending fine weather for harvest and protecting communities against their enemies. Gregory the Great, the same pope who had sent St Augustine to England, gave his authority to the doctrine known as the 'treasury of intercession', whereby the faithful were permitted to pray for special blessings through the mediation of the saints. The bodies of saints, such as St Cuthbert at Durham, came to be regarded as the chief treasures of the cathedrals and minsters where they lay. As it was believed that proximity to their mortal remains ensured a likelier chance of their former owners now in glory hearing the prayers made through them for intercession, so the places of their burial became points of connexion with the other worlds of hell, purgatory and heaven.

The remains of Anglo-Saxon cathedrals are few and generally tiny by comparison with their successors. Recent excavations at Winchester of the Saxon cathedral placed in one of the most important Anglo-Saxon cities, the capital of Wessex, have demonstrated that it did not cover a tenth of the area of the present cathedral. Although chroniclers such as Bede make much of the splendour of church building in their time and although ecclesiastics such as Benedict Biscop and St Wilfrid travelled to Italy where they were much influenced by what they saw, it is clear that builders and patrons lacked not only the technical skill to construct on a grander scale, but also the ambition. St Wilfrid built a cathedral at Selsey (the see was later removed to Chichester) and the crypts at Ripon and Hexham still remain of his works there, extraordinarily bare and poky culverts that, for all their simplicity, retain a numinous air and remind us of the crypts of the vast basilicas of Rome. For many reasons the early Irish churches are far more interesting than what remains of Anglo-Saxon building, both for the numbers that survive and for the skill they reveal in such features as their large-stone masonry.

A major change in the scale of cathedral building came about through the direct influence of the Normans, and behind them lay two great strengths. One was the Reform movement of the eleventh century whose centre was the great abbey of Cluny in Burgundy. The other was the revival of architecture through the widespread adoption of the Romanesque style. The two, in fact, travelled together, although the Reformers were working in Ireland well before the Anglo-Norman Conquest. The Reformers of Cluny saw the need to establish the priesthood as a separate and higher caste of humanity and to glorify the mass in the minds of the faithful. They demanded a literate and celibate clergy as obedient to the bishop as they in their abbeys were obedient

KILDARE: **a sixteenth-century tomb with** *(right)* **Christ as the Man of Sorrows**

to their abbots and priors. To fulfil their aims they needed buildings that in scale and adornment would proclaim the superiority of the sacerdotal class and increase the mystery and the otherworldliness associated with the sacrifice of the mass. They found what they needed in a new breed of masons and architects working in north Italy and parts of France in the late tenth and early eleventh centuries. These men were able to wield the skills, crafts and organizational abilities necessary to their profession to a degree unknown since the fall of the Roman Empire. They seem, too, to have been taken with the ambition to surpass the Romans in the sheer scale of their constructions. The Normans also appreciated the abilities of these masons for they needed them not only when they founded churches for the future repose of their souls, but also for the great keeps and halls of the castles they built to secure the possession of the lands they conquered.

The Normans in general worked very closely with the Reformers, who were disturbed at the state of the English Church. They induced the pope to give his backing to the invasion of 1066 and, when the Normans won England, all the English bishops except one, Wulstan at Worcester, were soon replaced by Norman, French and Italian ecclesiastics. Thus, at a blow both the native ecclesiastic and secular rulers were replaced by foreigners of a similar background and the bishops and the greater abbots were made vassals-in-chief of the crown. Another change followed that was to have far-reaching consequences: most of the Anglo-Saxon cathedrals had been run by secular canons, that is, priests living in a loosely knit community, though some, such as Worcester, were monastic foundations. Because the Reformers came from a monastic background, they converted the secular foundations of many of the great cathedrals to monastic forms, as in the cases of Canterbury and Winchester. This was an exception to the rule on the continent where cathedrals were staffed by chapters of canons – although the practice was also adopted in certain cases in Scotland and Ireland.

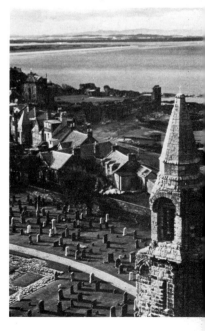

ST ANDREWS: **the south-east turret of the east wall, looking towards the Bishop's castle**

The Reformers also moved cathedrals, if they were in small villages, to larger centres of population. The see of what is now Norfolk moved from Elmham and Thetford to Norwich and that at Selsey to Chichester. Such moves were recommended by the Council of London in 1075. A little later, in 1109, the minster at Ely was elevated to cathedral status and the last of the English medieval dioceses was created at Carlisle in 1133 in country recently conquered from the Scots. The ancient Welsh sees of Bangor, St Davids, St Asaph and Llandaff were all refounded by the middle of the twelfth century, St Davids and Llandaff being under Norman influence, for the Normans penetrated the whole extent of the south coast of Wales to Pembrokeshire and St Davids. There they were poised for the conquest of Ireland. Ireland had already felt the force of the Reform movement and her dioceses were finally reorganized under the four archbishoprics of Armagh, Cashel, Dublin and Tuam in 1152. She had also received the influence of foreign craftsmen working in the Romanesque style, as at Cashel, and was able to draw on the rich traditions of Celtic ornamentation, as at Annaghdown and Clonfert. Cistercians and other continental orders displaced the older monastic ways and many of the higher church posts were given to foreigners. In Scotland, soon infiltrated by Norman adventurers who formed an alliance with the native Canmore dynasty, other dioceses were founded in addition to that at St

KIRKWALL: **exterior of the choir, south transept, and tower**

Andrews. We must not omit those outer regions which the Normans never mastered and which were controlled by their Norse cousins. There was a cathedral on the Isle of Man which looked after what were called the South Islands or the Hebrides (so that the Bishop of Man is still called Bishop of Sodor and Man, Sodor being a corruption of Sudray Ia or South Islands in Old Norse), and a cathedral in Orkney first on the tidal island of Birsay and then at Kirkwall.

The picture we then gain of events that influenced the cathedrals in the eleventh and twelfth centuries is one of immense change in the organization of the Church and in patronage. The Normans, on conquering England, were staggered by the wealth of the country; they at last possessed the means of exploiting to the full all the considerable advances in technology that had been made in various communities and parts of Europe during the Dark Ages. One result was their work on great cathedrals and abbeys to replace those of the Anglo-Saxons in the Romanesque style.

The Romanesque

The two immediately striking characteristics of the Romanesque style are the massiveness and stolidity of construction and the use of the round arch in bays, windows and decoration of arcades, together with rounded vaults and apses. Those characteristics were what tended to disappear as the Gothic style superseded the Romanesque. There were, however, other features affecting the basic form of the great church that were continued into the Gothic period. The first of these was that the church was constructed in the form of a cross and, therefore, in the shape of the body of Christ. The holiest part, representing the head and facing east, contains the sanctuary, the place of the high altar with the crypt extending beneath it where the relics were preserved. Often this part terminated in a rounded apse or groups of apsidal chapels but, because of the English preference for squared east fronts, only Peterborough retains much of its apsidal construction, although Gothic architects retained the form in rebuilding Norwich and Winchester. Moving west, we come to the point where the arms of the cross bisect, with generally a great tower rising from the columns of the crossing. Extending north and south from this are the transepts, the arms of the cross, each including their own entrances to the church. Then the nave, the largest unit, extends westward, so called because it is the *navis*, the ship of Christ. The nave exhibits a threefold division into its wide central part, generally roofed in wood, and its two aisles with stone vaulting. The laity were usually admitted only to the nave and were restricted to watching from the aisles because the centre was kept free for processions. The west front would contain three separate entrances, as at Lincoln, and these would be bordered by a pair of towers, as at Southwell.

The threefold division was also extended to the vertical design of the church. The first division is that of the piers and their bays which allow light from windows in the outer walls to penetrate into the ground level of the main body of the church. The vaults of the aisles are covered by tiled or lead-covered roofs that slope from the wall carried by the columns to the outer walls of the aisles. Over the vaults is the second stage of the design, the *triforium*, a word of unknown origin but first applied to this feature at Canterbury. Because arches are often cut in the triforium, at this stage a gallery is provided which is properly known as the tribune and which may extend nearly all round the nave, the transepts, the choir and the sanctuary. At great festivals the tribune may have been used for all those worshippers who could not be accommodated in the aisles, and magnificent hangings would be draped over the edge of the openings. It is a pity that this custom is now rarely observed because it would add much to the drama and excitement of important services. How to fit the triforium into the main vertical design of the interior was a constant challenge to the architects when they wanted to preserve the impression of height. Above the triforium rises the clerestory, which means the story that gives light above the roofs of the aisles, carrying the main roof or high vaulting of the church and containing the windows lighting the upper reaches of the building.

This threefold division illustrates how symbolism, in this case the symbolism of the Trinity, unites with practical considerations to make a satisfying design, capable of many variations, within the basic rules. It may be also that the architects were influenced by the neoplatonic ideas studied at the school associated with the cathedral at Chartres. According to these ideas the cosmos consists of a series of worlds, each, starting with the physical world, contained within another. The physical world is contained within the Soul of the World, which is itself contained within the Nous or the Divine Mind. All these worlds are ultimately dependent on the Creator. Thus, the foundations, columns and bays represented the physical world, the stage above that, the triforium, represented the Soul of the World and the clerestory represented the Divine Mind illuminated by the light of the sky. The idea of the church as the body of a man cannot, of course, be taken too far on the physical level. It has, however, psychological meanings, related to the neoplatonic ideas just mentioned, which affected the symbolism of nearly every part of the building. The stone, wood and glass of the physical cathedral represented the mystical body of Christ; piers and columns were interpreted as apostles and saints and glazed windows were the doctors of the church, letting in the light of true belief. The presbyteries and altars were the receptacles of the sacramental body of Christ and in the paintings and decorations of walls, vaults and roof depicting Christ ascending or on the Judgement Day the pilgrims were constantly reminded of His glorified body. In entering a cathedral, they were, therefore, passing into an artistic representation of the greatest ideal of humanity known to them and were allowed to circulate in aisles, passages and ambulatories that seemed like pathways into the mind of the highest intelligence.

However harshly the Normans might treat their conquered populations, they always showed the greatest respect to the cults and shrines of native saints, building great churches for them and so preserving much that was vital in the national memory. Through the commemoration of Anglo-Saxon saints such as St Erkenwald at Old St Paul's or St Werburgh at Chester and the similar veneration paid to Celtic saints such as St Blane at Dunblane in Scotland, ordinary people were kept close to their own history. When, however, the first crusaders conquered Jerusalem in 1099, they opened up to the West new ideas and new technological skills, undreamed-of riches of

DURHAM: in the north aisle of the nave – two drum piers, the nearer carved with chevrons, the further with diaper patterns on either side of a composite pier

decoration and texture to imitate and first-hand reports of the holy places. From these the cathedral builders could (in a composite manner) recreate their own holy city as a setting for the services, rites and dramas in which the events of the Gospels were re-enacted. The Normans with their international connexions could not resist the opportunity of imitating and trying to surpass the examples of continental, Byzantine and middle-eastern churches. In England, with almost one accord, they tore down the Anglo-Saxon cathedrals and abbey churches and replaced them with their new churches. Most of the cathedrals of this period were later on to be largely or wholly replaced by Gothic constructions, often because of fires and destruction. Of those remaining only St Albans, Rochester, Norwich, Peterborough and Durham are predominantly Norman work, though Chichester, Ely, Gloucester, Southwell and Winchester contain much that is important. What was probably the greatest building in terms of size was the nave of Old St Paul's in London, but that was lost in the Great Fire of 1666. The Norman minster at York, wholly replaced in the Gothic period, was even bigger than the cathedral of the same period at Canterbury.

In building these new cathedrals, perhaps because they were uncertain of what strains and stresses their columns and walls could take, the builders went for safety through piling on masses and through thickness of walls. They also adopted this style for other reasons: they wanted to make their great churches look like castles of the spirit that guarded true and permanent values, as opposed to the vaunting and transient ambitions of secular rulers. Another main effect in the interiors is of regularity, bestowed largely by the universal employment of the round arch so that naves, such as those at Ely or Norwich, seem to copy the immutable cycle of labour and prayer in the life of the monk, extending far ahead of the onlooker as the *opus Dei* extends into future history. It is not, however, a monotonous rhythm; it conveys the sense of a majestic similitude, and frequently the simpler the building, the greater its atmosphere of settled certainty.

Many of our modern impressions, though, of these churches are false, first of all because their interiors were extremely dark; their window openings, already proportionately small, were further diminished as sources of light by being filled with thick glass or with oiled linen. They must have been supremely extravagant in the use of candles and torches. Another more extraordinary fact is that large areas of their exteriors and interiors were coated in lime plaster and whitewashed. The plaster also provided the surface for the wall paintings and frescoes of which few traces remain but which, we know, were widely executed. These paintings were of many kinds: they included Christ in majesty depicted in the apses, as in St Gabriel's chapel at Canterbury, portrayals of the life of Christ set beside episodes from the Old Testament, as in the chapter house at Worcester, series of medallions, as in the nave roof at Ely (now a reconstruction of the last century), and bold overpaintings that picked out the geometric designs carved in the stone. This was done at Durham where the great cylindrical columns with their chevrons, lozenges and flutings were picked out in alternate bands of black and red. Lacking these painted surfaces, we tend to think of the Romanesque in these islands as a largely abstract art, an impression reinforced by the fact that so much of Romanesque carving that survives is confined to the abstract

ELY: **the Norman nave looking towards the octagon and the high altar**

forms of arcading, the interlacing of blind arches with which the builders gave interest to their walls. Only in a few instances does much figure carving survive, as in the west fronts at Lincoln and Rochester and in the series of crypt capitals at Canterbury.

It seems most likely that the English schemes of sculpture never achieved the scale and complexity of some of the Burgundian, Provençal and north Italian churches. It is, however, in the remaining sculpture that we find the chief challenge to the placid rhythms of the architectonic spirit of the Romanesque. An extraordinary number of the favourite themes of the sculptures concern battles and struggles between men and men, between men and animals and between animals and monsters. Why was this? If we look at the carved shafts of the Lincoln doorways, we find men and animals locked in the grasp of tendrilled branches and leaves as though life were a struggle against a malign vegetative spirit or as though man's spiritual aspirations could only be realized through victory over the delusive flowers and fruits of nature. If we study the capitals of the crypt at Canterbury, we are again in a nightmare world of battle and conflict. It is interesting, therefore, to turn to the Romanesque sculpture of Ireland where a totally different atmosphere prevails, an atmosphere of sane fantasy even when incorporated in the battered remains of a ruin like the cathedral at Annaghdown. There is another great difference in Ireland: the cathedrals and abbey churches were never built to the huge sizes of the great English churches of the period. Here the sculptors and architects could work better together to integrate their contributions into a single whole, as with Cormac's chapel or the west door of Clonfert. There is only one largely Romanesque cathedral remaining in what is now Scotland and that is Kirkwall on Orkney.

Even while some of the greatest churches in the Romanesque style were under construction, the style that was in a few years to supersede it utterly was already in preparation in the abbey of St Denis in the Île-de-France. England can boast in the nave vaulting of Durham the earliest known use of the pointed vault, but that, though obviously planned for from the inception of the nave, was the independent discovery of the unknown genius of that cathedral. As the twelfth century wore on, so there was a reaction against the massive and weighty designs of the earlier Romanesque, and a desire for greater elegance and lighter effects was manifested in the style known as Transitional because it bridges the Romanesque and Gothic periods. Among the most notable works of the Transitional style are the nave of St Davids, the Galilee chapel at Durham and the western bays of the nave of Worcester. The style lasted far longer in Ireland, particularly in the west as at Kilfenora and the chancel of Clonfert, long after the Gothic was firmly established at Dublin.

The Gothic style

The Gothic is essentially a creation of the Île-de-France, the region surrounding Paris which was the power base of the Capetian kings of France. Its chief characteristic is the pointed arch. Although, as we have noticed, there was a precocious use of the pointed arch in the vaulting at Durham, the true development of the style stems from the royal abbey church at St Đenis then on the outskirts of Paris where a great man, Suger, was made abbot in the early twelfth century. Suger was not only an important politician and organizer; he was a patron of exquisite taste. Deeply influenced by the writings then attributed to Dionysius the Areopagite, the Athenian converted by St Paul, whom he believed to be identical with the St Denis whose relics lay in his abbey, he passionately believed in the power of beauty to elevate the mind to God. This is a passage he wrote describing what happened to him when he contemplated works of art:

> When – out of my delight in the beauty of the house of God – the loveliness of the many-coloured stones has called me away from the external cares, and worthy meditation has induced me to reflect, transferring that which is material to that which is immaterial, on the diversity of the sacred virtues: then it seems to me that I see myself dwelling, as it were, in some strange region of the universe which neither exists entirely in the slime of the earth nor entirely in the purity of Heaven; and that by the grace of God, I can be transported from this inferior to that higher world in an anagogical manner.

'Anagogical' is a term applied to the highest reaches of contemplation, a state the great Gothic cathedrals seem to refer to in every part because the symbolical meaning of the pointed arch is the aspiration of the soul to God. The pointed arch combines this association with considerable practical advantages over the rounded arch of the Romanesque. It is strong structurally because it makes greater use of the opposition of forces, and it is more efficient in the distribution of stress. By employing it, the architects of the Gothic were able to construct churches of greater height, with thinner walls provided with greater intervals both in the bays between columns and in the proportion of wall area that could be devoted to windows. This meant that the cathedrals could be opened to the influx of light and that light itself could be used in their adornment in the great expanses given to stained glass. Glass was to become a primary building material, instead of a decorative extra.

A fifteenth-century lyric says, 'As the sun that shines through glass, So Jesus in his mother was'. From Christ's words 'I am the Light of the World' there grew a tradition of thought according to which the physical light by which we perceive our surroundings is only a pale shadow of the divine light on which the former depends for its existence. From the words of St John, 'In him was life and the life was the light of men', derived the understanding that this divine light was the possession of all. Influential works, such as those of Dionysius the Areopagite already mentioned, developed these ideas and represented them as the emanations of God working through the hierarchies of angels. All things were disposed by God in weight, number and measure, and the Deity was depicted sometimes with a pair of dividers as the Great Architect. The symbolism of light led to the apportioning of meanings to the various colours which would always be used according to their proper signification. The idea that all things in nature were disposed according to number and proportion and that everything had a number whose meaning expressed its individuality was another inspiration to the architects. The most obvious use of number symbolism is in three, the number of the Trinity, but a thirteenth-century work by the French bishop, Guillaume Durand, sets out number symbolism related to all parts of a church. Again it was probably the teachings on proportions that were regarded as the secrets of a mason's lodge and which would vary according to the nation or the region of the lodge (as their particular guild associations were called). Such teachings were not just rules of thumb for setting out the proportions of a building, but were related to a full understanding of their cosmological significance.

It is in the Gothic architects' attitude to light that we can see their new style as a creation of the north. The Romanesque style derived from Roman models and from a southern climate where it was the aim of builders to exclude strong sunlight and provide cool interiors. International though the Romanesque as a Christian architectural style was, it could never with its limited window space feed the hunger of the north for light. The main elements of the Gothic style – the pointed arch, the ribbed vault and the flying buttress – which were the inventions making possible this new light-filled interior, were not isolated technical discoveries. They were, in fact, the culmination of a long and immensely important technological revolution in northern Europe that began in the Dark Ages with inventions and introductions such as the heavy plough which released the energy stored in the alluvial river basins of the north-west or the stirrup that helped to make possible the conquering cavalry of chivalric society. Amongst the masters of the new technology were the monks of the Cistercian order who chose the wildest and most secluded places for their settlements, where they practised self-sufficiency. They established their monasteries in England, Scotland and Wales in the twelfth century, reaching Ireland in 1142, and they were the first to bring the elements of the Gothic into these islands. They were attracted to the style because of the efficiency of construction but, by the rules of their order forbidding any but the simplest decoration of their churches, they could not make use of its decorative possibilities. It was when the monks of Canterbury, after the choir of the cathedral had suffered a disastrous fire in 1174, called in the French architect, William of Sens (a story told in greater detail on *page 42*), that the new style received the highest possible patronage and the authority that secured its general adoption throughout these islands. Its advantages were seen with such speed that Wells, the first cathedral in Europe to be built with the pointed arch throughout, was being constructed only a few years after William of Sens had started his work at Canterbury.

The Romanesque cathedrals had expressed the aims of the powerful Benedictine orders, especially that of Cluny, with all the fervour of the Reform movement. The Gothic is essentially a secular movement, drawing on the new professional groupings in the towns for their higher standards of execution and style, and though, of course, the architects and craftsmen were still dependent on great ecclesiastics for their patrons, these were frequently prince-bishops who were involved to the hilt in the political life of their times. The period of the Gothic cathedral builders covers roughly 350 years. There are certain constants that ensured that, for all the variety of styles within this period, it forms a complete artistic period. One of these is the adherence of the Church to the Western Catholic tradition with an episcopacy and with religious foundations that required the construction, or the extension, of great churches. This means that the patrons remained roughly the same:

WELLS: **the high altar and east window with the prospect of the retrochoir and Lady chapel beyond**

bishops and the deans and chapters of secular foundations and the priors and monks of monastic cathedrals, supported at times by members of the royal family and great noblemen. When the bishops were abolished or changed their functions in the sixteenth century, the age of the cathedral ended.

The makers

Another constant was the organization and ideals of the architect-masons. In building a great church they were helped by a variety of skilled craftsmen, organized for the most part in guilds or trade organizations – carpenters, joiners, skilled carvers in wood, glaziers, smiths of all kinds working in iron, lead, brass, bronze, silver and gold, stoneworkers ranging from the men in the quarries to the carvers of the figure sculptures, painters, sailors and bargemen who brought the cut stone and wood by water, waggon drivers whose oxen dragged the materials to sites not so fortunate in possessing navigable rivers, as well as the clerks of works, fund-raisers, sellers of indulgences and importunate patrons. One example of the enormous masses to be shifted was Salisbury Cathedral, built mainly between 1220 and 1286 with thirty years in the next century for the tower and spire: it required 50,000 tons of Chilmark stone, 15,000 tons of Purbeck marble, 3,500 tons of oak (most of this hidden because it supported the roof above the vaulting) and 400 tons of lead. Salisbury was built in a very short period; most other cathedrals took far longer to reach their complete state. This meant that it could be rare for an architect to see the completion of even a part of a cathedral in his lifetime. This, in turn, meant the necessity of a lasting brotherhood amongst the masons to transmit the skills and secrets of the lodges from one generation to another and to foster the development of local styles.

The architects in charge of the design of a great building were obviously much admired and much sought after. They were needed and consulted as military engineers as well as for the construction of palaces and castles; since the prestige of kings and prelates depended so much on the ostentation of their surroundings, these mason-architects were highly esteemed and rewarded. What is curious about them as a group is that, although we may know their names, what they built and how much they and the craftsmen working under them were paid, we know very little about any one of them as a personality. Let us take, for example, one of the greatest, Henry Yeveley, master of the works to Richard II and the creator of the nave of Westminster Abbey, the Neville screen at Durham and the nave of Canterbury. No chronicler worked to perpetuate the quirks of his nature as they did for his tragic or brutal patrons. No pupil made notes for posterity of his moments of inspiration or his methods of working. Yet, it is clear that he, like so many of his predecessors and successors, was one of the most eminent men in the kingdom. The very mystery of their half-anonymity may reveal the key to the surpassing excellence of their creations. Their brotherhood of art secured a general high standard of craftsmanship and allowed to flourish the geniuses who devised the new styles of succeeding fashions. They surrendered the memory of individual fame in the record of petty idiosyncrasies to the greater memory contained in lasting works of art. What we know of them, we know

SALISBURY: **the spire and eastern portions**

in the present moment when we visit their buildings because what was greatest and best in them is carved into the stone about us. What we can say of them when we are in the Angel Choir of Lincoln, or gaze westwards from the Lady chapel of Wells, or study the spire of Salisbury, is that they included men of stupendous imaginative power and intellectual vigour, who had the skill, capacity, administrative ability and will to make these works of art convey the ecstasy and the insights of their inspirations.

Viewed as a group devoted to the expression of certain ideals through their art, they give the impression of men who had to keep themselves apart from life, not out of hatred of sex or from fear of sin, as in the case of many of the gloomier clerics of the time, but for the better fulfilment of their aims. The men who could carry in their heads the final profiles that Lincoln or Cashel should present to the traveller while as yet unfinished were men marked with a separate fate. They were as far advanced in civilization beyond their contemporaries as in earlier times the saints we have mentioned and whose shrines they adorned outshone the barbaric Saxon, Pictish and Celtic tribes to which they brought Christianity. We have only to read the Orkneyinga Saga for the period in which Kirkwall was built with its unrelenting sequence of murder and rapine and then to look at the cathedral which the masons from Durham constructed to understand that they had skills and ideals far different from those about them and their patrons. The cathedrals they constructed allowed the rapid development of other forms of art, not only in the plastic arts, but also in music, as with the school of Notre Dame, and in drama. In many ways they were religious and philosophical innovators. The new conception of man as an immortal individual was first expressed in the figure sculpture of Chartres and was soon to be followed in England at Wells, many years before the scholastic philosophers started to debate the nature of the individual soul and to damn their opponents' souls as they did so. The delight in the variety of human character shown by Chaucer in the later fourteenth century had already appeared over a century earlier at Lincoln, a cathedral he must have known well. No illustrated botanical book of the time shows the realism and attention to detail of the leaf sculptures of the Decorated period, as at Southwell or Lincoln. Such precision in observation was one of the main ways in which Western science was to find itself.

As the cathedrals were the greatest technical achievements of the Middle Ages in the sense that, of all the constructions of the time apart from military engineering, they demanded the highest ingenuity in engineering skills, in the deployment of vast masses of materials and in the invention of techniques to move them, then it follows that the development of Western technology can be ascribed to a high degree to the cathedral builders.

Construction

Any addition to a cathedral or renewal of its fabric first required consultation between the patrons and the architects. Sometimes, as at Canterbury in 1174, a group of masons was brought together before one was chosen to carry out the work – in this case William of Sens. With the rise of a school of architects associated with the royal court in England from the thirteenth century onwards, the king's masons would often be consulted even when

LINCOLN: **part of the triforium of the Angel Choir**

SOUTHWELL: *(left to right)* **hawthorn, maple and buttercup leaves on the capitals to the left of the chapter house portal**

they were not carrying out the commission themselves. The patrons would rebuild and add to their fabrics for many reasons – because part of the older work had fallen down, because of fire, because of changes in ritual, because they had acquired new and important relics and they needed to attract more pilgrims or because they had the funds and simply wanted to make new and splendid buildings. Edward I in 1297 ordered inventories to be taken of church treasures with a view to confiscating them, should he need the funds for war against France. This is thought to have been the reason for the switch in the fourteenth century to investing in immovable buildings rather than in portable jewels and goldsmith's work.

The architect would visit the site and study the local quarries. Sometimes, even if the stone was locally available, there was not the trained labour force to excavate and cut it. For long after the Conquest stone imported from Caen was used in many southern English buildings and the Somerset masons who built Christ Church, Dublin, shipped their native limestone across the Irish Sea in preference to local stone. When the general design was agreed upon, the next stage would be in the drawing office. If much sculpture was planned for the commission, then the architect would consult an ecclesiastical adviser; for example, the mason, Nicholas of Ely, worked with Elias of Dereham at Salisbury, and James Winter, the carver, worked with Alexander Galloway on the design of the nave ceiling at Aberdeen. They would work together not only on iconographic schemes for decoration, but to make sure the ritual needs of the canons or monks were fully satisfied. One of the most obvious changes brought about by new devotional movements was the provision of Lady chapels, because of the growing cult of the Virgin Mary from the twelfth century onwards. Once all the elements of the design had been agreed, the templates would be cut which acted as the guides for the moulding of columns, voussoirs for arches and tracery for arcading and windows. As much as possible of the stone-cutting would be done at the quarries to save transport costs. If the building was wholly new or was to extend beyond the older foundations, foundations would be laid to accord with the orientation of the church or cathedral, i.e. to make sure that the long axis of the building faced due east and west. From studies carried out in Oxfordshire and elsewhere it appears that the orientation of a church was found by watching for the point of sunrise on the day of the saint to whom the new church would be dedicated. Sometimes the site would cause difficulties; at Lichfield the Lady chapel veers out of alignment because of the ridge on which the cathedral is built. At Glasgow the extreme slope of the valley resulted in the brilliant solution of lower and upper churches in the thirteenth-century rebuilding of the cathedral.

Soon after the first courses of the walls arose and the bases of the columns had been set, the architect would have to bring in scaffolders, cranes and other hoisting machines and carpenters. Once the oxen and draught horses had brought the stone to the site, every piece had to be put in place by human muscle-power, using block and tackle pulleys and cranes. One great advance in the thirteenth century was the invention of the wheelbarrow. Another was the great improvement in carpentry skills in the early Gothic period over the Romanesque. The accuracy with which an arch was constructed depended on the carpenters who made the centering, the wooden framework which held all the voussoirs of an arch in place until they locked together on completion. Similar constructions were necessary for the lights and tracery of mullioned windows, for flying buttresses that took the thrust of high clerestories and for every section of stone vaulting. As one bay was completed, so the centering could be taken down and used for the next bay. Beyond this there was no possibility of prefabrication. Every framework had

CANTERBURY: **centering in use in the reconstruction of an arch in the cloisters**

to be designed and made for its particular job. Craftsmen in both stone and wood derived great benefits from improvements in metallurgy: their tools were stronger and more reliable. The monks at Canterbury were amazed to see the capitals of their new choir being carved with chisels instead of axes. The use of the chisel allowed much deeper undercutting of the stone.

As the walls rose, so the cranes would be jacked up for the next course of masonry. Where there was a wide enough base as in the building of a tower, the cranes would be worked by treadmill wheels, which are depicted in several manuscript illuminations. Much of the work was highly dangerous – as William of Sens's accident at Canterbury (*page* 42) demonstrates – and required exceptional powers of attention and alertness on the part of the workers. Once the walls reached their ultimate height, in England at any rate, the wooden roof would be constructed. The frame set up by the carpenters called for plumbers, or leadworkers, who would unroll and fix the sheets of roofing lead, ridging them in patterns to counteract the tendency of lead to slip. Under the cover now provided the stonework of the high vaulting could proceed. This must have been one of the most arduous and demanding of all tasks. First the wooden centering would have to be mounted on scaffolding. This would, as far as possible, conform to the desired shape of the vault. Then earth would be poured on the frame and moulded into the form of the vault. Each section of the ribs which had been carved below would then be hoisted up and set in the earth like an open cage, linking in with their bosses. These bosses, which seem so small when viewed from below, are often several feet in diameter. If, as at Norwich where there are 225 bosses in the nave vaulting, they formed part of an intricate iconographical scheme, the slightest damage in transit could have added weeks to the building programme while a new boss was carved. As the Gothic period progressed, so the design of stone vaulting became gradually more intricate, moving from the comparatively simple ribbed vaulting of Durham, in which every rib springs from a shaft in the side walls to the fourteenth-century lierne vaulting, and, later, to the magnificent complexities of designs like the choir vault of Oxford. With the cage of ribs and bosses in place, the interstices would be filled with thin stonework; then the earth and some of the framework would be removed to allow the painters to decorate the bosses, ribs and panels. When they had finished, the scaffolding would be dismantled and re-erected for the next bay.

As each stage of the building was finished, so other craftsmen moved in to carry out their embellishments, the painters, the metalworkers, the tilers, and the glaziers. All the time the works were going on, the monks or canons would have had to carry on their services in whatever part of the cathedral was free from building activities or was completed. Finally there would come a day when the cathedral would be considered finished and it would be consecrated – as on the great occasion in 1318 when, in the presence of Robert Bruce and all the higher clergy and nobility of Scotland, St Andrews was consecrated, an occasion that must have set the seal on the long struggle for national independence.

This is necessarily a short and composite picture of the main stages in constructing a cathedral, but what is said here applies in general to the whole period of Gothic architecture whose various styles are now described.

overleaf, left: PETERBOROUGH: **the Norman south transept with the Victorian central tower**

overleaf, right: LICHFIELD: **the 'Ladies of the Vale' – the three spires illuminated by night**

The styles of the Gothic

The names given to the various styles of Gothic in England are those devised by Thomas Rickman early in the last century. The three main styles are Early English (1175 – the rebuilding of Canterbury – to 1265), Decorated (1250 – the rebuilding of Westminster Abbey by Henry III – to 1350) and Perpendicular (1330 – the chapter house of Old St Paul's and the new work at Gloucester – to 1540). These names can also be applied to contemporary or similar work in Scotland and Ireland – though they are also distinguished by other terms such as first or second pointed, or early Irish Gothic. Each of these styles overlaps with the one preceding it, as is natural in the rise of fashions, and each has its own subdivisions. Early English is distinguished between the styles of Canterbury and Wells and the later mature work of Salisbury and the chapel of the Nine Altars at Durham. The Decorated begins with the rich ornamentation of the Angel Choir at Lincoln and the angular geometric style of the nave at Lichfield; it develops into later stages known as curvilinear and flowing. The Perpendicular is sometimes given a subdivision called Tudor for late buildings such as Bath Abbey.

Early English is the style of the first half of the thirteenth century, the time of St Francis and St Dominic, when their followers, giving the lead to scholastic endeavour, attempted to bring all knowledge into the service of faith through the aid of reason. There is something about the Early English style that is eminently sane and reasonable; it has the strength and the elegance of clear thought. For the first time, apart from Durham, the builders felt capable of building stone vaults for their naves so that the whole interior of a cathedral was bound together into a unity by the use of the same material. The ribs of the vaulting are nearly always functional; they are never included, as happened later, for the sake of decoration. The characteristic window shape of the style is the lancet, so named because of its resemblance to a lance or spearhead. These were slender, tall lights whose internal divisions were provided by the metal frame of the glazing. The finest examples to retain their original glass are the Five Sisters windows of York, although to appreciate the simple beauty this form could attain one can turn to some of the Irish ruins such as Ardfert. The use of stone mullions and tracery came later in the century.

What is clear is that almost from the beginning there was an attempt to create a separate English style of the Gothic and there were specific ways in which English cathedrals were to develop. One of these was in the proportion of length to height; no English cathedral attains the nave heights of the French or some German cathedrals, but on the other hand they surpass their continental sisters in length. Of the Scottish cathedrals Elgin, which is comparatively short, shows a strong French influence and only St Andrews began to compete in length with the English cathedrals. But in their case, as with those of Ireland, they were smaller because their populations were poorer. Another peculiarity is in the design of the east ends; where French cathedrals carried on the rounded apsidal tradition of the Romanesque, the architects in England preferred the squared east ends which provided so much more light than the rounded French chevets. This again affected Scotland and Ireland and produced the effect peculiar to these islands of the

ELGIN: **tombs in the south choir aisle with the west towers and window beyond**

light-flooded east end, a feature that has been attributed to the longer survival here than elsewhere of pagan sun worship. Another explanation can be found in the use of Christian sun symbolism by the medieval mystics and in number symbolism.

In the course of the thirteenth century the Early English style developed under the influence of Rheims into what is called the Geometric style, as in the nave of Lichfield and the north transept of Hereford. This allowed for windows of much greater area by the provision of stone mullions repeating the motif of the pointed arch and by the use of geometrical patterns, such as trefoils and quatrefoils, in the tracery. Surface areas, such as in the spandrels between arches, were now also decorated with raised tracery where before they would have been frescoed or whitewashed. This was a further development of the Gothic spirit, the impulse to make a building a complete work of sculpture, so that whether the decorative features are figures, leaf or flower patterns or geometrical figures, they are not intermittent intrusions on the architectonic scheme, but organic parts both of the body and the soul of the great church. Two of our early Gothic cathedrals, Wells and Lincoln, already illustrate this admirably in their exteriors as well as within. The

screen of the west front of Wells, with its remaining figure sculptures set in niches of the buttresses and wall faces, reveals the influence of the great iconographic schemes of the French cathedrals, where at Chartres and later at Rheims an astonishing revolution in the ability to sculpt recognizably individual and lifelike human forms had already announced a new age in Western civilization.

Much English work has been lost through the depredations of the Reformation, the weather and ignorant restorers. Of what remains, much of its original effect is lost because it was brilliantly painted in gold and bright colours. Nevertheless, the exterior of Lincoln's nave, transepts and choir with their countless faces, angels and demons, each a tiny part of the immense whole but accumulatively giving an impression of rich diversity, illustrates one aspect of the Gothic spirit: joy in the manifestations of life. The screen of Wells illustrates another: how the depiction of men and women as impressive individuals grew out of their being considered as parts of an overall historical and cosmographical pattern. The niches in which they stand are not just convenient open hutches to protect them from the worst of the weather, but, with their hoods and columns, they are extensions of the lives of the saints and prophets they enclose. The niche expresses at once the place of a holy man in creation and in Christian history and the extension of his soul across time and space in the reticulation of other lives.

Among the new possibilities of the Gothic, with the development in craftsmen of greater technical skills, was the provision of great buildings for the monks or canons of the cathedrals where they could conduct their business or their studies. Among these are the beautiful series of polygonal chapter houses, such as those at Lincoln, Westminster Abbey, Salisbury, Wells, York and Elgin, and the great cloisters where the new skill in making larger window areas through the use of stone mullions led to the building of pointed and traceried stone arcades through which the religious could gaze on the pleasant garths beside their cathedrals.

CANTERBURY: **a view across Henry Yeveley's cloisters**

The Decorated style covers the period from about 1250 to 1350, a hundred years of extraordinarily ambitious building, a period of greater height and vertical thrust, of ever more elaborate vaulting, of stunningly complex ornamentation, especially in the use of leaf patterns, and of great structural advances. The windows grew and grew to take up more and more of the wall space, the churches were ever more opened up to light and the dark crypt-obsessed spirit of the Romanesque was abolished by a new, fearless spirit evinced by the desire to erect buildings of spectacular virtuosity. To this period belong works such as Exeter Cathedral almost in its entirety, the eastern portions of Wells and the chapter house, the nave and the glorious west front of York Minster, important additions at Lincoln including the central tower, the octagon and other works at Ely, most of Lichfield, the choir of Bristol and the east window of Carlisle.

Then, in the course of the fourteenth century, the Perpendicular style, named after its emphasis on verticality but with many other special characteristics, was introduced. It first appeared in St Stephen's chapel at Westminster and in the chapter house of Old St Paul's in about 1330, but was soon adopted on a grand scale in the new works at Gloucester, where the abbot had to provide a fitting setting for the tomb of the recently murdered

King Edward II. The style was a creation wholly original to England. While the English in the course of the Hundred Years War wrought the devastation on France that virtually brought the period of cathedral building to a close in that country, they were able in the more settled conditions at home to continue to extend and adorn their cathedrals. In many ways, the Perpendicular led to a more abstract and logical form of architecture than that of the Decorated period; above all it was a style in which the window triumphed over the wall, in that wider and wider expanses were devoted to glass, and the design and tracery of the windows determined the design of the traceried blind panels of the wall surfaces. Among the works of exceptional originality, the greatest is Henry Yeveley's nave at Canterbury. This latter time also saw the completion of many earlier cathedrals with the provision of grand central towers: Worcester, Gloucester, Wells, Durham, York and Canterbury and, in Wales, St Davids. It was also a period of embellishment of cathedrals in the provision of richly carved stalls, in the erection of elaborate chantry chapels like miniature churches within the cathedral, and of the use of heraldry as a language of decoration.

YORK: **beasts and faces in the frieze below the parapet of the west front**

Though there were additions to several Irish cathedrals in the Perpendicular style, none of these shows either its adaptation to a national style, except perhaps in tomb sculpture, or any works on a grand scale. The most interesting ecclesiastical buildings of this later period are often the friary buildings of the mendicant orders which we cannot discuss here. The unsettled political and social life of Ireland at this time militated against great programmes of construction and the bishops who were appointed from England never in many cases got to their sees to organize new building works.

This could not be said of Scotland where enough remains to show the development of a truly national style, drawing on the French *flamboyant* style and on the Low Countries for influences in this later period, but also harking back to certain Romanesque forms for inspiration. This last point can be seen in the drum piers of Aberdeen and Iona. Another influence bringing in a certain grimness of aspect was from castle building in the provision of strong fortified towers, as at Aberdeen and Brechin. To counter this, however, was the ingenuity the architects displayed in the rich curves of their tracery and in creations as original and beautiful as the crown on the tower of St Giles.

opposite top left: BRISTOL: **arches and transverse vaults in the south aisle of the choir** *top right:* ST DAVIDS: **panels and pendants of the Tudor wooden ceiling of the nave** *below:* CANTERBURY: **a view of the nave vaulting showing also clerestory windows and the blind tracery beneath them**

The end of the period

One important aspect of our ancient cathedrals is that in them we feel the living presence of history – something that is brought out further in the discussions of individual cathedrals that follow. Many of the smaller cathedrals of Scotland and Ireland, frequently because of their isolation and associations, preserve an atmosphere that brings us closer to the time of their construction and the spirit that animated their builders and patrons. Others, nearer to the centres of power, are more alive with the ghosts of those who played a part in the drama of the Reformation. Thus, the tomb of Prince Arthur at Worcester recalls his early death and the marriage of his wife, Catharine of Aragon, to Henry VIII. The divorced Catharine is buried at Peterborough. The marriage of her daughter, Mary, to Philip II of Spain took place at Winchester in the presence of the courts of England and Spain – the marriage that failed to produce a Catholic heir for England. At Norwich the shields of the Boleyn family figure prominently near the high altar and in the cloisters, from which the monks had been driven only a few years before, Elizabeth I was royally entertained in 1578. The presence of John Knox broods over St Giles and St Andrews – and in the ruins of Cashel we remember Elizabeth I's trimming archbishop, Myler McGrath, who read the English service in the cathedral while a fugitive priest said mass for his wife and children in a secret chamber above.

THE ROCK OF CASHEL: **the cathedral seen from the east within its 'cashel' or perimeter wall**

Bath

THE ABBEY CHURCH AT BATH cannot be called a cathedral in any strict sense, although it stands on the site of earlier buildings that certainly deserved the name. The Bishop of Wells, however, is the Bishop of Bath and Wells, a title that reflects the earlier shuttling of bishops, undecided as to which town to make their see. All good buildings partake in the spirit of their environments, and the spirit of Bath is health. Even the fittest visitor to Bath finds somehow that he feels that much better, and one of the finest tonics administered there is the sight of the west front of the abbey approached by the paved courtyard of shops, with the Pump Room on one side. Soaring up on the turrets bordering the great west window are two ladders carved with angels descending and ascending. This refers to the story of the abbey's complete rebuilding by Oliver King, secretary to Henry VII and Bishop of Bath and Wells. He had a dream, like Jacob, of angels going up and down a ladder and a voice said 'Let a King restore the Church'. The old Norman church was completely removed, except for an insignificant arch, and the work began in

below left: **The exterior of the tower, north transept and part of the nave**

below centre: **The west front: the ladders with angels can be seen on the turrets**

The rebus of Bishop Oliver King, the builder of Bath Abbey – An Olive tree growing through a King's crown

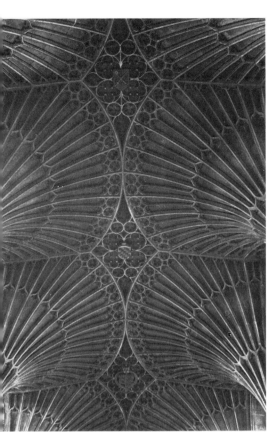

Fan vaulting in the nave: Victorian work that faithfully follows the pattern set by the Vertue brothers in the choir

The east window and high altar seen from the choir

1499 under the famous masons, Robert and William Vertue, the architects of Henry VII's chapel at Westminster. They promised Bishop King vaulting that would be finer than anything in France or England. Although the church was unfinished by the time of the dissolution of the monasteries, the fan vaulting of the chancel and the side aisles had fortunately been erected. The crossing of the tower was vaulted under Elizabeth I, but the nave did not receive its fan vaulting until the last century. Luckily the pattern had been set and was followed extremely skilfully so that the impression of the interior is of a great architectural unity. The eye is caught by these lovely half-goblet shapes, like the under-leaves of tropical fronds, and delights in the rounded rhythms each fan makes with another. This prepares us for another aesthetic shock : we are kept looking up all the time so that in coming to the arches of the crossing to the transepts, the building seems to take a leap into the air and become even higher. This effect is obtained by the fact that the transepts are much narrower than the nave and chancel making the tower above the crossing rectangular and not square. The later history of Bath as the resort of rich invalids is evident everywhere along the walls of the aisles. In no other place, it would appear from reading the inscriptions, were the bones of so many virtuous, noble and courageous persons congregated together as here.

Bristol

BRISTOL was one of the six abbey churches raised to cathedral status by Henry VIII in 1542. Up to the dissolution it had been a foundation of Augustinian canons started by Robert Fitzharding in 1140. As Bristol was the greatest port of late medieval England and one of the richest cities, it had long deserved its separate status as a diocese. The cathedral was much altered and rebuilt in the last century. The nave with its west front is wholly the work of George Edmund Street (1868-88). From the cathedral's earliest days, little survives of Norman work except for the chapter house and its vestibule of about 1150-70, with stone vaults and richly decorated arcadings and mouldings. What declares the originality of the cathedral and reflects the international importance of the medieval city in which it was created is the chancel and its aisles, which, together with the attendant Lady chapel, were begun in 1298 and finished by 1330. As the aisles rise to the same height as the choir, it is a type of church more usual in late German Gothic, known as the hall-church. In the games of surprise which all good architects play with space it is a great development because it reveals a further aspect of the Gothic spirit: shafting and overarching of light combining with the effect of a forest in always suggesting prospects and glades beyond. The overarching effect is provided by the vaults of the aisles which, being at right angles to the choir-vault, rise up and then zoom down to rest on the centres of bridges, which are set across the aisles, before rising again to come down on the facing wall. The bridges themselves are pierced, thus adding to the lightness of the effect made by the abolition of the triforium. It is this that makes the chancel itself so lithe and spare with its lierne vaulting – amongst the earliest examples in the world – rising from delicate corbels that are all the trace left here of the capitals an earlier designer would have insisted on providing.

Even if one wanted more after such a delight, this cathedral has little to offer of the same standard. It has charming carvings in what is called the Elder Lady chapel beside the north aisle of the chancel built by Abbot David about 1210 (who asked the Dean of Wells for workmen to carve the columns); it has the chapel of the great local family, the Berkeleys, and the Lady chapel proper that extends beyond the chancel with a much restored Jesse window which acts as the east window of the cathedral as a whole; and it also possesses a late Anglo-Saxon carving of Christ at the Harrowing of Hell.

Anglo-Saxon carving c1000 of the Harrowing of Hell

A view eastwards from the choir showing the early lierne vaulting

Canterbury

CANTERBURY is as rich and as grand in its variety and its dimensions as befits the see of the Primate of All England and as the goal of the greatest English pilgrimage route of the Middle Ages – the tomb of Thomas à Becket, martyred in the cathedral in 1170. The pre-eminence of Canterbury, however, extends far beyond the time of Becket, since it was here that the missionary, St Augustine, sent by Pope Gregory the Great, converted Ethelbert, the pagan king of the Jutes, in AD 597. A detailed written description remains of the Saxon cathedral but virtually nothing else, because after the Norman Conquest Archbishop Lanfranc and his successor, Anselm, rebuilt it on a much grander scale. This work was in its turn largely replaced by later building, although the shell of the choir, the eastern transepts with the south-eastern tower and the quite remarkable crypt with its superb romanesque carvings survive.

It was to this, now largely vanished, Norman cathedral that Thomas à Becket returned in 1170 from exile caused by quarrels with his former friend, King Henry II. It was in the north transept of the crossing that four knights, provoked by an angry outburst of the king at Becket's defiance of him, hacked him to death. When his monks came to unrobe his body, they found that for

below left: **The east end of the cathedral showing the exterior of the choir, the Trinity chapel and** *(right)* **the corona or Becket's crown**

The south choir transept with its adjoining tower: part of Anselm's Romanesque cathedral

The nave from the steps of the crossing

The crypt of the Trinity chapel by William the Englishman

years he had been wearing a hair shirt which was swarming with lice. They realized that a saint had been amongst them – an opinion confirmed both by the penance Henry II performed at his tomb, when the monks of the cathedral flagellated him, and by the extraordinary number of miracles that were ascribed to Becket's intervention. Shortly after his death, a great fire gutted the choir and so provided the opportunity for rebuilding it and extending the cathedral eastwards to make a worthy setting for the shrine for such a saint

Lot's wife turned to the pillar of salt, a detail from a thirteenth-century window in the north aisle of the choir

and martyr. The monks called together French and English masons and were so impressed by the intelligence and reputation of one man, William of Sens, that they settled for him. It was a momentous choice because, although certain Cistercian abbeys in the north had already introduced elements of the new style from France, William of Sens, by employing here the early Gothic style of the cathedrals of the Île-de-France, ensured that Canterbury, as a result of its prestige throughout England, would encourage a general tendency for all English churches to follow the Gothic style. The monks had hoped to preserve as much as possible of the Norman building, but gradually William of Sens brought them round to the view that it had to go.

Work on the new choir proceeded fast from 1175 to 1179. Then in that last year, as William of Sens was supervising work on the vault over the high altar, he fell from the scaffolding and was so badly injured that he had to resign his post. He was succeeded by William the Englishman, who was responsible for the Trinity chapel where Becket's shrine was to be placed, the crypt beneath it and the circular chapel at the far east end known as Becket's crown or the *corona*. By raising the Trinity chapel above the level of the choir, he completed the feeling of a triumphal ascension evoked by the successive flights of stairs that lead the pilgrim up from the level of the nave.

The shrine of Becket was installed in 1220, and for generations it attracted crowds of pilgrims to pray and offer gifts. The journey along the Pilgrim's Way from London inspired Chaucer to write *The Canterbury Tales*. One of the chief attractions of the cult of Becket was that he symbolized resistance to tyrannical authority; it was this that made Henry VIII so determined to root out devotion to his name. By 1538, when Henry VIII's commissioners destroyed the shrine, so much had accrued to it that twenty-six wagons were needed to bear away the offerings and objects associated with the cult. Now all that remains is the magnificent pavement laid before it with its design of

One of the sequence of English kings in the pulpitum

opposite: The nave: a view eastwards of Henry Yeveley's masterpiece

quatrefoil, lozenges and roundels. The other survival of this period of the cathedral's decoration is one of its exceptional glories – the glass. Most of it is now in other windows than those for which it was originally designed, although it is known that it was all designed and placed according to a central and guiding programme. In recent years it has been attacked by the poisonous fumes of modern transport and industry. At the time of writing, a programme of restoration restricting access is under way. Nevertheless, there are few aesthetic experiences in Britain to compare with the exhilaration and delight of moving along the aisles of the choir into the eastern transepts and round the ambulatory of the Trinity chapel, and of watching the flaming reds and deep brilliant blues, flecked with greens and yellows, resolve themselves through rounded patterns into noble patriarchs and saints and sequences of miracles.

The Black Prince was buried here in a magnificent tomb in 1363 and his Chantry chapel was constructed in the crypt. The most important fourteenth-century work was the new nave. Lanfranc's Norman nave and transepts survived many changes to the rest of the cathedral till the later fourteenth century when Prior Hathbrand decided to rebuild them. The designer was Henry Yeveley, the greatest architect of late medieval England. He had to keep to the width and length of the doomed Norman nave, but was not restricted by height, so that he pitched his nave to the height of the chancel. To enter the nave is like intruding into a great banqueting hall where the true guests awaiting the feast are the sixteen gigantic columns, their shafts encasing the Norman work and soaring up to meet in the bosses of the vault. The work began in 1378 with the building of the aisle walls with their huge windows. The central arcade and the clerestory, begun in 1391, were the crowning glory of Yeveley's long life. The nave of Canterbury is serenely perfect. For all its great height and the emphasis on the vertical thrust of the shafts of those tremendous columns, it is a profoundly peaceful work of art. The ample windows of the aisles let the light pour through into the central space in sheets of radiance over the floor and the swathes of vaulting effloresce from their shafts, as though nothing could be more natural or easy to accomplish. Yeveley, who was also responsible for the new south transept and the cloisters, died in 1400 before the nave was finished in 1405. The work was continued by his pupil, Stephen Lote, whose other works here include the pulpitum with its clinically severe statues of kings, and Thomas Mapilton, who also replaced the Norman south-west tower (1424–34). The Norman north-west tower was rebuilt in the early nineteenth century to make it symmetrical with Mapilton's tower. The north transept was rebuilt in the mid fifteenth century, but Richard Beke, the architect, was careful to preserve the sacred site of the martyrdom. Then, in the last years of the great works of the cathedrals, Canterbury was given the central 'Bell Harry' tower, begun by Thomas Wastell in 1496. He placed fretted strainer arches on two sides of the crossing to strengthen the columns supporting it below and then raised the tower with octagonal corners ascending to spired open lanterns in a design that perfectly combines strength with elegance. The height of the tower counterbalances the vast length of the cathedral and asserts its spiritual authority over miles of the surrounding countryside.

Carlisle

THE STARTLING RED SANDSTONE EXTERIOR of Carlisle with its battered tower and fragmentary nave looks more like one of the ruined castles of the neighbouring border country than a sister of the more gently reared cathedrals of the south. It suffered particularly badly in the Civil Wars when General Leslie's soldiers reduced most of the Norman nave to ruins. As a result of these depredations the interior of the cathedral is quite curious when one enters by the south transept door. Only two bays remain of the simple Norman nave built by the secular canons who founded it as a collegiate church in 1092 and who were soon supplanted by Augustinian regular canons from 1123 onwards. Because it is cut short, it looks like an altarless chancel facing the wrong way. There is no view into the choir because it is completely masked by the organ and its screen with a curious dog-legged entrance. The tower and transepts are fifteenth-century, dark and undistinguished, so that the entry into the choir by one of the aisles with their ornate early Renaissance ironwork screens is something totally unexpected. Here is a richly ornamented hall, containing at one end some magnificent choir stalls, delicately sculpted capitals to the pillars and, as the culmination to this guarded treasurehouse, the great east window, often considered to be the finest existing example of decorated tracery. The aisles of the choir were built between 1245 and 1292, but the main body of it was not completed until the end of the fourteenth century. Two great architects were possibly involved, Ivo de Ragheton who also worked on the west front of York (he would have been responsible for the east window) and John Lewyn, a noted builder of castles.

Every trace of history in the country surrounding Carlisle seems to recall an endless cycle of tragedy and savagery. Inside the choir the contrast is so great as to make clearer than almost anywhere else the special gift the makers of the Gothic brought to medieval man: the vision of life whose product was beauty and spiritual calm and not vengeance or destruction. The works of the twelve seasons carved in the capitals of the choir remind men of the peaceful round of agriculture so often disrupted in that region by war, the smooth curving to a point of the arches of the bays suggests the aim of the contemplative life and the nine tall lights of the east window reflect the emanations of the nine orders of angels pouring down on humanity the blessings of the Trinity, expressed through the multiple intricacies of the tracery.

above: **The choir, showing the tracery of the great east window** *and left:* **One of the series of carvings depicting the seasons in the capitals of the choir**

Chester

CHESTER IS SO ANCIENT and so finely sited a city, with so much remaining of all periods of its history from Roman times to the present age, that it is a pity that its cathedral is not quite worthy of the approaches and surroundings. This is not to say that it lacks features of outstanding interest because, as we shall see, it contains many; but both inside and out it is a jumble of ancient decay and heavy Victorian restoration, lacking, except from certain views, in grandeur and beauty. Like Carlisle, Chester is a red sandstone monster, with a tower of largely nineteenth-century work (Gilbert Scott) and a west front partly masked by another building. Although it attempts the cruciform plan, its north transept, the only remaining Norman work apart from the north tower and part of the cloister, is much smaller than the south transept of about 1340, and its nave is too wide in comparison with the first and too short to match the second. The vaulting is of wood and the north aisle of the nave suffers from vast and vapid mosaics of the last century.

Bench ends and canopies of the choir stalls

The church began as a foundation of Saxon secular canons who built a shrine for the early saint, Werburgh, a lady of impeccable descent, being the daughter of the king of Mercia and related to three other royal families. Chester was one of the great strategic points of the Norman Conquest and a bishopric was set up in the city for a short time in the late eleventh century, based not here but in the surviving church of St John. The cathedral was raised to its present status by Henry VIII, having been in the possession of Benedictines from 1093 to 1540. It is on entering the choir, the work of Richard Lenginour (1272–1314), that we find work of the quality that is so missing from the parts already mentioned, first in the stonework of the arches of the triforium and then in the glorious woodwork of the choir stalls with their fretted and spired canopies or tabernacles, bench ends and misericords. This woodwork, dated about 1380, is amongst the finest in the land, equalled, if not surpassed, only by Lincoln and, perhaps, Beverley. Here the monks would have stood like saints in their niches, their voices carried by the sounding boards of the panelling behind them and the aspirations of their souls given visible form in the leafy, crocketed spires that rise in two layers above their seats to form a city of pinnacles ranging round the forty-eight stalls. There is hardly a legend or story of the Middle Ages that did not contribute a theme to the carving of the misericords and the bench ends: the Bible, the Arthurian legends, the Alexander cycle, Aesop's fables, travellers' stories of fabulous monsters and, of course, St Werburgh. Passing beyond the high altar we find her shrine, much restored, but still with the niches in which the sick rested their heads all night while waiting for her compassion on their suffering. It stands in the elegant Lady chapel built between 1265 and 1290. Much also remains of the conventual buildings of the abbey, including the cloisters

Details of misericords: *above:*
Samson and the lion *and below:*
A green man

**The east walk of the cloister,
showing the entrance to the
chapter house vestibule**

(greatly restored in part), the refectory with its elaborate stone pulpit and the
chapter house. Of these, the most exciting building is the little vestibule to the
chapter house, a square room with its stone vaulting supported by four
shafted pillars without capitals so that the shafts run straight up to form the
ribs of the vaulting – though the chapter house itself, stone vaulted and with
lancet windows, is a work of admirable proportions.

Chichester

CHICHESTER WAS FOUNDED as a see in 1075 when the bishop removed there from Selsey, the site on the coast from which St Wilfrid had begun the conversion of the south Saxons. One of the finest views of this appealing cathedral is gained by approaching it across the flat country from Selsey and seeing its spire clear against the distant high wall of the South Downs. The present building consists largely of Norman work constructed in the course of the twelfth century, though this is frequently modified by, or encased in, later work. The twelfth-century builders had to contend with two great fires, the second of which destroyed much of the older east end and led to the building of the present retrochoir, one of the most important remaining examples of early Gothic work. The immediate impression of the nave, which was originally constructed in two phases (the eastern bays between 1114 and 1123, and the western bays by 1148) is one of considerable simplicity. Then, in the thirteenth century, the wooden roof was replaced with stone vaulting, borne on slim, triple shafts that rise from the flat, inner facing sides of the piers. A closer inspection from the aisles reveals a greater complexity in the construction because, unusually, these are double aisles formed when chapels extending outwards were incorporated into the aisles themselves, thus providing a pleasing feeling of spaciousness. The Gothic treatment given to the Chichester nave demonstrates both in the adaptation of the bay design to the provision of stone vaulting and in the construction of the aisles how tactful and economical the masters of the new style could be when they were required to marry older works to new demands.

The master of the retrochoir, Walter of Coventry, had a freer hand because of the extensive damage caused by fire and, though obviously influenced by

The inner aisle on the north side of the nave

Carving in the triforium arcade of the retrochoir: an angel emerging from a trefoil in the spandrel

The Norman nave with its thirteenth-century vaulting: a view eastwards showing the Arundel screen

below: **Purbeck marble shafts on piers of the Early English retrochoir**

the work recently carried out by William of Sens in the neighbouring see of Canterbury, he employed the English solution of the square east end which now leads to a charming Lady chapel of the Decorated period. A great furtherer of building here was Richard of Wych (bishop 1245–53), better known as St Richard of Chichester, whose shrine once stood behind the reredos. In his time the tower was built, later to be capped by a spire around 1400. Other notable features of this later period are the Arundel screen, or pulpitum, restored to its old position before the choir in recent years, the oddly irregular cloisters and the free-standing bell-tower to the north-west of the cathedral, a unique example of its kind. The most memorable feature of Chichester, however, is its spire which in its present state is entirely Victorian. The old one collapsed on 17 February 1861 at half-past one: the fall was expected and a contemporary account says: 'the spire was seen to incline slightly to the south-west, then to descend perpendicularly into the church, as one telescope tube slides into another, the mass of the tower crumbling beneath it'. Gilbert Scott, called in to restore the spire, was fortunately able to draw on much recorded material, and what we see now is one of the most successful reconstructions of the period and one that fully preserves the intentions of John Mason, the original architect.

Durham

DURHAM CATHEDRAL is one of those supreme buildings by which all others of its kind are classed. Built on a site that has challenged architectural geniuses over centuries to their finest efforts, it stands on a high peninsula looped about by the broad river Wear. Wooded about its lower slopes and centred in the long line of the medieval citadel, with a great castle guarding the land approach and the main part of its monastic complex surviving and nestled by streets of old houses, Durham offers an infinity of views. These, whether from the surrounding hills, from the riverside or the bridges, from sudden vistas in the town or in the perambulation of its hilltop, always draw the gaze with magnetic power to its west towers, whose open lancets in various aspects show the sky beyond, and to the great central tower that rises like a shout of triumph from the heart of humanity to heaven. As few other buildings are, Durham is a living presence, the evidence in stone of men who made conquests of the intellect, heart and will in regions of human capacity of which it is one of the purposes of great art to remind us. To persuade us that such capacities exist we have the life of St Cuthbert written by the Venerable Bede recording the holiness of the patron saint of Durham, and we have the evidence of almost superhuman inspiration in the cathedral itself.

Cuthbert's body, miraculously incorrupt, was brought to Durham in AD 995, more than a century after it had been taken from Lindisfarne on wanderings to seek safety from the Danes. The monks, having been told by Cuthbert in a vision to seek the Dunholme, happened to hear a milkmaid speak of it as the place where a cow had strayed. This was the sign that they had found their new home. They soon built what was to be known as the White Church of which only admiring descriptions remain. William the

right: **The view of the west front and the towers from across the river Wear: the exterior of the Galilee chapel can be seen extending from the west front**

The cathedral after sunset

Conqueror, having to put down serious rebellions in the north-east, built the castle, and the earldom of Northumberland was transferred to the first Norman bishop of Durham. So important was Durham, first for the settlement of England and also as a bulwark against the Scots, that the bishopric of Durham became a great territorial lordship with all kinds of special rights and privileges. It was in the time of the second Norman bishop, William of St Carileph, that the present cathedral was begun. He had the White Church pulled down and the new choir was built between 1093 and 1099. After his death and in the time of his successor, the wicked Ranulph Flambard, the nave was largely built and the whole was completed by 1133 with the stone vaulting of the nave, thus making it perhaps the greatest Romanesque church in all Europe.

One of the special joys of Durham is that the interior is the equal of its outside. Very often in other cathedrals, either because of depredations or because of uneven levels of skill, one aspect is superior to another, but at Durham, even after the aesthetic delight of its towers and grandiose form, the first sight of the nave with its alternation of composite piers and great drum columns is astounding. Each pier, from which the main arches of the vaulting rise, seems to speak with the voice of God out of the whirlwind to Job, 'Where wast thou when I laid the foundations of the earth?' Every rounded column, answering pattern to pattern across the nave and up into the transepts and choir, with fluting, chevrons, hatching and swirling bands, continues the urgent questions that stun us into a sense of the smallness of our usual conceptions. The bold patterns of the columns are replaced in the arches of the arcades and then of the triforium with mouldings that seem, taken with the scale of the whole, of extraordinary delicacy, as though the intention of the builder was that, once the onlooker had been overpowered by the first impression of the nave, then as he gazed upwards he should be rewarded and comforted by the gentle undulations of the rounded arches. Above all rises that stone vault with the earliest pointed arches to announce the coming of the Gothic. All three main elements of the Gothic style are present in this work at Durham – the pointed arch, the ribbed vault, and the flying buttress – although here the flying buttresses are hidden above the aisle vaults. The whole – choir, transepts, nave, vaulting and lower stages of the west towers – was completed in forty years; the architect or architects are unknown.

The growing practice of veneration of the Virgin led to the provision of Lady chapels in the course of the twelfth century. When, under Bishop Hugh du Puiset, Richard the Engineer tried to build a Lady chapel in the customary place at the east end, the foundations slipped and the walls cracked. This was attributed to the intervention of St Cuthbert who did not want women coming close to his shrine which had stood behind the high altar since 1109. So the Lady chapel was built at the west end in about 1170 and is now known as the Galilee, a lovely, low rectangular church with its arches zigzagged like rondures of lightning, supported by shafts of Purbeck marble. The Galilee, probably so named because it was there that a great procession commemorating the return of Christ to Galilee ended, is Transitional.

The Gothic came comparatively late to Durham after its precocious beginnings, first in the upper stages of the west towers of about 1220 which have lost their spires, but in other ways retain their singular beauty, and then

The central tower and the north transept

Part of the east wall of the chapel of the Nine Altars

A vaulting bay of the nave

The view eastwards of the nave

in the construction of the chapel of the Nine Altars behind the high altar and about the shrine of St Cuthbert. Approaching this chapel from the choir aisles, one descends, instead of rising up as at Canterbury, and it gives an impression of an immense gain in height, an impression strengthened by the tall Purbeck shafts that stand free of the windows and the wall arcading. This highly unusual longitudinal space, extending on both sides like transepts from the main body of the cathedral, is a creation of awe-inspiring richness, for all the dreariness of the Victorian glass which now occupies the windows. It was the work of Richard Farnham from 1242 onwards and was designed to be as impressive as possible an approach to St Cuthbert's shrine, to which one mounts on a platform. Here St Cuthbert is still buried. Henry VIII's commissioners on coming to despoil his shrine were amazed to find the body of the saint who died in AD 687 still undecayed in 1540. Remarkable finds taken from his coffin in the last century are displayed in the upper library. Between the shrine and the high altar stands the reredos, designed by the great Henry Yeveley, which formerly held over a hundred alabaster figures. It is known as the Neville reredos after the famous Northern family who largely paid for it. Much of the damage carried out by despoilers in the Reformation and also by starving Scots imprisoned in the cathedral after the battle of Dunbar in 1650 can never be repaired, but Bishop Cosin, made bishop at the restoration of Charles II, provided the magnificent choir stalls and the canopy of the font.

Amongst the medieval later works we must mention the extraordinary domed kitchen built between 1366 and 1371 by John Lewyn, who later designed the cloister with Thomas Mapilton. And perhaps as wonderful as any aspect of earlier work is the great central tower built in two stages (1465–75 by Thomas Burton and 1483–90 by John Bell the Younger) with its saints descending from heaven to earth in the niches of its angled buttresses, the aspiring ogees of its windows, and the view of miles and miles of northern hills it affords to those with strong legs and sound wind who reach the top.

Ely

ONCE THE MONASTERY and cathedral of Ely stood on an island in the fens. Now the waters have receded and the cathedral can be seen for miles standing on its high mound across the flat, green fields. The history of the church is very ancient; founded by St Etheldreda in AD 673, it was sacked by the Danes in AD 870 and later reconsecrated. The first Norman abbot, Simeon, began in 1083 to rebuild the choir and central tower which, for reasons given below, no longer exist. In 1109, during the period of construction of the major part of the present building, Ely was made a bishopric and the abbey church its cathedral. What the visitor first sees from far off is the extraordinary west tower which is part of an unusual complex called the west transept, consisting originally of north and south projections with octagonal arcaded

opposite: **The Norman nave looking towards the octagon and the high altar**

right: **The high altar and the lancets of the eastern end**

Nodding ogee arches in the arcade of the Lady chapel

corner towers and with the west tower in the centre. Unfortunately, the northern section fell down in the fifteenth century, so we lose much of the original screen effect it might have presented. Windows, polygonal forms, incuttings and overhangs, shafting, arcades and blind arcades, all these are used to create a welcoming feeling as though the monks and architect had chosen to play with the form of the castle while deliberately rejecting its defensive and frightening nature. The tower and west transept are of the later twelfth century, with two major additions, the Galilee porch of about 1250 and the lantern on the tower, formerly crowned with a lead spire, of about 1400.

Once inside, the eye sweeps through the immensely long Norman nave which marches on for twelve bays. Its extreme regularity makes it a good example of how the life of those under obedience, the monks, was expressed in architecture. It must also be remembered that it was the processional way along which, in a splendour of vestments and jewels, the monks would issue from their closed-off quarter of the church beyond the crossing to delight the waiting faithful on important holy days. To us now it is a processional way in the opposite direction because it leads to one of the most original achievements of the Gothic in England – the octagon of Ely.

In February 1322 the Norman central tower fell down, severely damaging the choir as it did so. The sacrist of the time, Alan of Walsingham, who was responsible for the fabric of the cathedral, was, according to the Ely chronicler writing later in the century, at first overcome with despair before having the stones and wreckage cleared away. He had foundations dug and measured out an octagonal scheme whereby eight columns were to rise to support the new roof. Alan was one of those cultivated clerics of whom we recognize other examples in Elias of Dereham at Salisbury and Matthew Paris at St Albans, who played a great part in the design and decoration of their respective churches. How far Alan was responsible for the design of the scheme is difficult to say; in any case he had to work with a master mason and a master carpenter, who was William Hurle, the most distinguished carpenter of his age. Influences on the possible design have been sought as far away as Persia, and Sir Nikolaus Pevsner has suggested the hexagonal crossing of Siena Cathedral as a possible source. In its design, function and technical construction the Ely octagon is unique. It consists of four great arches for the cardinal points of the crossing, each linked to the other by a scheme in the diagonals of arcade arch, blind triforium and large, sharply-pointed windows. The vaulting rises from shafts at each of the eight angles but, instead of meeting in a central boss or pillar as in the octagonal chapter houses in other cathedrals, it halts to rise again in the lantern which seems to rest lightly upon the wall of the vaulting. The lantern, which is of wood and is supported by a largely hidden construction (possibly the earliest use of the hammer-beam principle) is so oriented that each of its eight angles faces a straight side of the octagon beneath it – it is twisted round, in fact, to add a new subtlety to the design both inside and out. The eight windows of the lantern are surmounted by a star vault with a figure of Christ in the central vault.

The whole design is something of uplifting beauty. Light shafts down from the windows of the diagonals of the octagon and is also held in the lantern,

The west tower, Galilee porch and south-west transept

Looking up into the lantern of
the octagon

A view across the octagon
showing *(left)* the choir and
(right) the south-east side

suspended like an aureole above our heads. If we were to name the spirit of
the octagon, we might call it 'the new life' because that is one of the symbolic
connexions of the number eight on which the design is based. Eight
symbolizes the balance between the powers of the spirit and the powers of
nature. At this period of building it was particularly connected with baptism
– which is why so many fonts are octagonal – and with regeneration. When
we recall that the Ely octagon is the result of recovery from a great disaster to
the cathedral, we can see how such a theme of regeneration would naturally
appeal both to patrons and artists.

The first three bays of the choir destroyed in that disaster were also rebuilt
at the same time. Beyond them extends the thirteenth-century presbytery
built by Hugh of Northwold between 1234 and 1252. Alan of Walsingham
had planned a Lady chapel even before the fall of the tower; this was
postponed and completed after the octagon. It is placed in the north-east
corner of the transept and choir and contains the remains of some of the
richest decoration of the period – much damaged in the course of the
Reformation.

Exeter

EXETER IS THE PRIME EXAMPLE of a cathedral of the Decorated period. Although what capture the eye first of all, especially when seen from the approach from the estuary of the river Exe, are the two Norman towers that, unusually, rise from the transepts and not from the west front, the present building was almost entirely rebuilt in the century after 1275. Exeter began as a bishopric in 1049 when the see was moved down-river from Crediton. At the same time with the unfortunate suppression of the Cornish see of St Germans, the power of the bishops of Exeter stretched to take in the whole of the south-west peninsula. It was unfortunate because it deprived the Cornish of the chance to make a great cathedral of their own, a lack which was not made good in the last century with the building of Truro. With a tithe of the mining revenues of Cornwall going to the bishops, Exeter was a very rich see, and under certain bishops, several of whom held high office at court, the cathedral was rebuilt to its present form. Among these was Bishop Stapledon

below left: **The west front with its screen of statues; on the right is the southern tower of the two Norman transept towers**

Head of a king on the west front

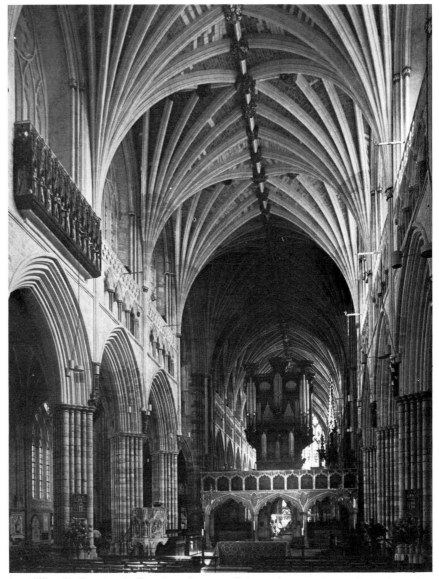

The nave with the pulpitum and organ: the minstrels' gallery can be seen on the left

who became Lord High Treasurer to Edward II and was murdered in the streets of London for his loyalty to that monarch. He gave munificently from his own money to the reconstruction of the cathedral. Among other examples of his bounty is the founding of Exeter College, Oxford.

The reconstruction had begun probably under Bishop Branscombe in about 1275 with the building of the Lady chapel and the retrochoir. This was followed in the period between 1288 and 1308 by the presbytery and the choir. The architect for much of this period was Roger of Exeter, who may have been the originator of the whole scheme and who set the pattern for the extension of the work in the nave. The nave was built by Thomas Witney (1328–42) and it was vaulted by Richard Farleigh, the architect of Salisbury

Angels playing instruments in the Minstrels' gallery

spire, between 1352 and 1369. In spite of the long period of rebuilding and reconstruction, these later architects were faithful to the main elements of the design in the presbytery, thus achieving the exceptional unity which the interior of the cathedral presents to the eye. The vaulting with its luxuriant ribbing extends, uninterrupted by a central tower, for 300 feet, the longest stone vault in these islands. Its richness is anticipated in the shafting of the piers; there are sixteen shafts to each pier, combining together like voices in unison. The vaulting shafts rise from corbels carved as baskets of flowers and leafage set immediately above the capitals. Much of their carving is particularly fine, as is that of the bosses and of the pulpitum which was given by Bishop Stapledon in 1324. Under him too was begun the bishop's throne, a startling creation, almost a cathedral in itself, with a canopy rising to a height of 57 feet. One of the many delightful features of the interior is the minstrel's gallery which replaces the triforium stage above a bay on the north side. It has fourteen angels, each carrying different musical instruments, and its presence here seems to symbolize a conscious aim on the part of the masons of Exeter to produce in the spectator that particular and miraculous singing in the mind that certain architectural effects can achieve, the sense that architecture is itself 'frozen music' as the German Romantic, August von Schlegel, once described it.

The date of the gallery is not certain, but it was probably erected at the same time as a far more ambitious programme, the addition of a screen to the recently finished west front, designed by William Joy and carried out between 1346 and 1375. This had the effect of making the west front step back in three planes – screen, façade, with the west window and embattlements, and then the nave roof behind. Massive figures of kings, prophets and saints, far too big in scale for the screen in which they are placed, stand, sit cross-legged or lean out of windows, their worn faces weary with history.

The pulpitum, a view showing elaborate foliage in the spandrels of the arches and the series of paintings framed in stone above

Gloucester

GLOUCESTER, one of the great mitred abbeys of England, was made a cathedral by Henry VIII in 1540. It owes much of its present splendour to the courageous abbot, Thoky, who buried in his abbey church the mutilated body of Edward II, murdered in Berkeley Castle on the orders of his wife, Isabella, and her lover, Roger Mortimer. The abbot of Bristol had refused to accept the corpse, and so had two other abbeys, but Thoky took it in and the unfortunate monarch's tomb, splendidly furnished by his son, Edward III, became a shrine visited by countless pilgrims. Their motives may have been no purer than those of the habitués of murder trials today, but the wealth they offered was partly used to reconstruct much of the Norman church. First in the transepts, choir and Lady chapel, then in the tower, the west front and the cloisters, the monks of Gloucester commissioned some of the greatest works of the Perpendicular style.

Gloucester had been a monastic site since early Saxon times and is first mentioned in AD 681. The building of the Norman church began in 1089 and though the east end is much altered, the original plan survives in the crypt. The nave was probably finished by the consecration year of 1121 and follows a pattern also employed at Tewkesbury and the now destroyed Evesham and

below centre: **The Norman ambulatory of the choir with Edward II's tomb on the right**

below right: **A view of the crossing showing the bridges carrying the vaulting shafts**

The tomb of Edward II

Pershore in the use of great cylindrical columns. At Gloucester these are so immense in relation to the width of the nave and the diminutive triforium that their inspiration seems to owe more to an earlier epoch of history, to the megalith builders of Stonehenge, rather than to the slimmer columns of Roman temples and basilicas to which they are more nearly related. They are an awe-inspiring sight, in many ways more so now than in early times when they were brightly decorated with reds, greens and yellows. The vault above them is mid thirteenth-century work, much needed in this particular church because Gloucester was especially subject to the great fires that swept through the wooden roofs of so many Norman churches. This formidable and naked nave is blocked off from the choir by a pulpitum and organ loft that permits only a glimpse of the decorative wonders beyond. Once past it, however, and in the choir we are in the presence of the largest east window of medieval England.

The new work at Gloucester had begun on the south transept in 1331, shortly after Edward II's body had been received there. The next task was to remodel the Norman choir which had been built to a different design from the nave and contained a deep triforium and gallery stage with wide openings. Walter Ramsey, the architect who is generally held responsible for the introduction of the Perpendicular style in the chapter house of Old St Paul's, probably came to Gloucester to advise on the new design of the choir. The solution adopted was not to pull down the Norman work, but to clothe it in

Norman drum piers in the nave, with a glimpse of the thirteenth-century vault

Ball-flower decoration on a window of the south aisle of the nave

new masonry. Few buildings demonstrate better than Gloucester the fundamental contrast between Romanesque and late Gothic architecture; the former seems to have been planned from the foundations upwards, the latter from the topmost bosses and the clerestory windows downwards. Thus, here the masons incorporated the Norman gallery and bays into the overall design, not only by the thrusting shafts masking the Norman piers and extending right up between the clerestory windows, but by bringing the tracery pattern established in those windows downwards in wall panels and in the tracery that acts as a grille over the Norman arches. The east window which is the chief glory of this light-filled interior, retaining much of its old glass, was built between 1347 and 1350; it is said to celebrate the victory of Crecy in 1347. As the masons worked westward on the vaulting, they came to the crossing and, wishing to carry the same design across, they built the most elegant arches across the gaps to the transepts, so that the vaults beneath the tower could spring from the same height as their fellows.

Gloucester was again to be in the vanguard of fashion in the early fifteenth century, when the cloisters with the new feature of the fan vault were completed. Another great work was the building of the central tower in about 1450. Owing much to the earlier and neighbour tower at Worcester, it is a spectacular sight on a fine day, shining white against the clear Cotswold sky which beams through the latticed parapet and the tall cages of the spired corner turrets.

Hereford

HEREFORD suffered a great disaster in the eighteenth century. The tall, single tower that stood at the west end collapsed in 1786 on to the Norman nave, reducing much of it to rubble. James Wyatt was invited to redesign the west front and the damaged nave. In doing so, he did away with the old triforium and introduced a new design of his own, cutting off the shafts which formerly ran from the piers to the roof. Despite his works and those of later restorers, Hereford is a small, but charming, cathedral to which the visitor comes already medievalized, so to speak, by the extraordinary richness of its surrounding countryside in churches and castles. Naturally, the cathedral shares in this wealth of historical and spiritual associations. It was founded in Saxon times round the shrine of St Ethelbert, a king of East Anglia, murdered by his overlord, Offa. One of Ethelbert's teeth was preserved there and regarded with great veneration in the Middle Ages. The usual Norman rebuilding took place in the period 1074–1145, and, apart from the rebuilding already mentioned, much remains in the choir, crypt, south transept and the

below left: **North-western view showing the double-storied north porch, the tower and the west front totally rebuilt after the collapse in 1786**

The font and Norman piers in the nave

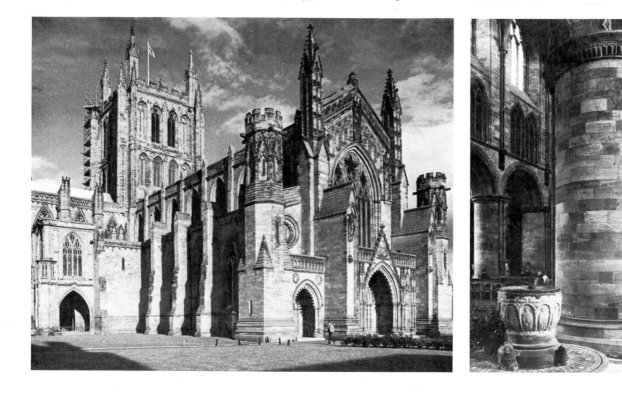

Geometric arches in the
triforium of the north transept

The north transept

nave. The Lady chapel is an addition of 1217–25, an aisleless hall notable
chiefly for the thick clustering of shafts in the window embrasures and the
fine series of lancet windows above the altar. Hereford was then brought to
the forefront of fashion by the Savoyard bishop, Peter Acquablanca, a protégé
of Henry III, who, obviously influenced by his master's works at Westminster
Abbey, built the astonishing north transept. It is the most extreme example of
that phase of the Decorated style known as the Geometric. The arches are
almost straight-sided, giving a triangular effect both in the bays and the
triforium; the effect is sharp, memorable and disturbing. A tomb in fitting
style was provided here for Acquablanca on his death in 1268. One of his
successors as bishop was Thomas de Cantilupe, a prelate noted equally for his
piety and his litigiousness, both against local magnates and his archbishop at
Canterbury. Shortly after his death in 1282 a remarkable series of miracles
were associated with his remains. He was soon canonized and apparently
was good for curing animals as well as humans. Edward I used to send his sick
falcons to be healed at his shrine, which was set up in the north transept in
1287. The base of his shrine still stands there, ornamented with figures of
knights templars because Cantilupe was their provincial Grand Master in
England.

Apart from this transept, the most notable and attractive feature of
Hereford is the central tower, built about 1315. A bold, massive square tower,
richly covered in that local decorative delight, ball-flower ornament, it used,
until 1790, to carry its original spire of lead-sheathed wood. Unfortunately,
this was removed and the corner pinnacles erected a few years later. One of
the saddest losses is that of the decagonal chapter house (1359–76), which is
thought to have been vaulted with the earliest examples of fan vaulting. Now
only the entrance and a small part remain.

Lichfield

WANTONLY DAMAGED AND HEAVILY RESTORED, Lichfield is, nevertheless, one of the loveliest cathedrals. With its three spires, the 'Ladies of the Vale', exercising a gentle rule over the town and country nearby and set in an intimate close of fine seventeenth- and eighteenth-century buildings with prospects over pools of water, it preserves a spirit that is absolutely individual in its quietude. It is the church of St Chad, bishop of the Mercians AD 669–72, to whose shrine here there was a pilgrimage. Being a sandstone cathedral, it has suffered the usual drawbacks of that material, as well as depredations in the Civil War when successive waves of soldiery from both sides besieged it or used it as barracks or stables. The central spire collapsed and was rebuilt in the seventeenth century and again in the 1740s; the two spires, the west front and much of the interior were heavily restored in the last century. Hardly a statue on its exterior is original, and yet in its profile and in the main features of its dispositions it is a pure expression of the Gothic spirit.

The west front in itself is extraordinary. It is a screen with the two west spires placed on it at either end and the screen is studded with big figures. Whereas other screen fronts such as Lincoln or Peterborough invite you in through great indentations and shadowed inlets to doorways and whereas at Wells, for example, the figures are housed in canopied niches, here the invitation is offered by the statues jutting out from the smooth wall as though they were advancing to meet the visitor. It does not matter particularly that the present figures are dull or insipid Victorian work; they too will decay and perhaps a future age will find the sculptors to replace them with worthier examples. The point is that the architectural intention is preserved and the figures advance towards us as though declaring the mystery of how the individual soul arises out of the invisible world represented by the smooth stone behind them.

Once inside, the nave, though heavily restored by James Wyatt and by Gilbert Scott, presents the impression of a great intellectual achievement. This is the masterwork of the Geometric style and it is marvellously proportioned, in arcade, triforium and clerestory, 2:1:1. There is a strong, but light, vertical movement in the thin shafts rising from the columns through cinquefoils in the spandrels and up to the vault springings which enclose the curved triangular clerestory windows also to be seen at Westminster and Hereford. There is a rolling rhythm in the horizontal direction conveyed by the wheel-like forms of trefoils in the clerestory tracery, quatrefoils in the tracery of the triforium arcades and the cinquefoils in the spandrels between the bays. Here, surely, we can see the influence of numerology on design, the Trinity in the triple trefoils, four in the quatrefoils expressing 3 + 1 – the

The nave looking eastwards to the high altar and, beyond, the windows of the Lady chapel

The west front by night showing the rows of statues

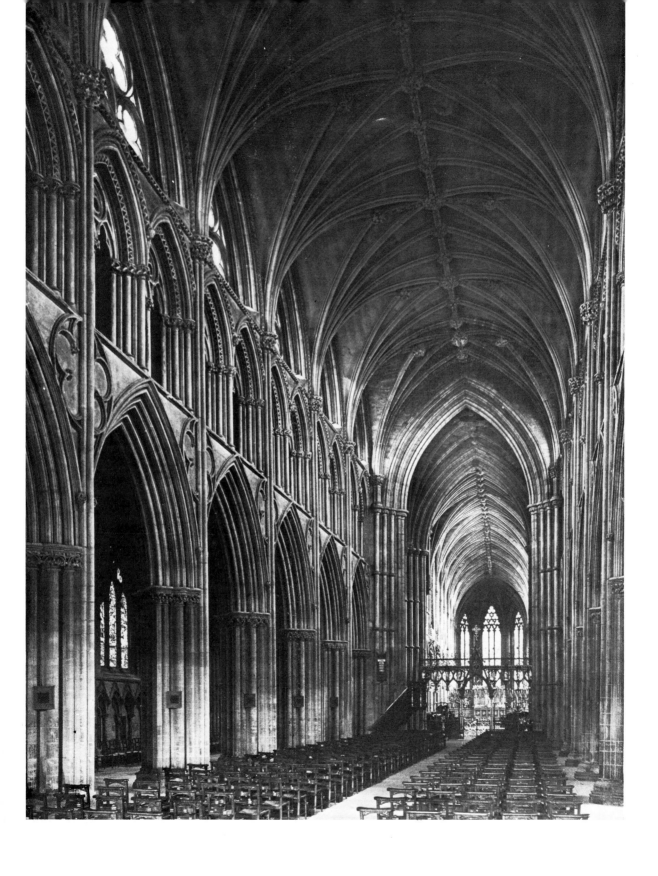

Trinity and what it acts upon, the world – and five in the cinquefoils, the number of man, of love and of the cycles of generation. The main shafts cut through the cinquefoils as though bearing down to earth the emanations of the spiritual world and infusing the march of time with the omnipresence of eternity. This nave was possibly the work of William FitzThomas and Thomas Wallace between 1265 and 1293. Its rolling rhythm carries us up to the crossing and the early thirteenth-century work of the arcades of the choir. The clerestory windows of the choir are seventeenth-century Perpendicular, put in after the spire collapsed. The crossing, which links nave and choir with the massed shafts of its piers bound at intervals by annulets (little rings) as though they were gigantic bundles of rods, again startles us into recognition of intellectual power. As in so many cathedrals, at the point of the crossing we are forced to reflect on the power of four, the number of the universe, of wholeness of meaning, of settled laws on which solidity and endurance depend.

From the north choir aisle we are led by a vestibule, itself one of the special charms of Lichfield with its wealth of carved arcades and seats where the poor sat while their feet were washed, into the chapter house, one of the more unusual polygonal buildings of its type. It is eight-sided, but two of its sides are longer than the others, giving the impression that it should have been decagonal as the ten shafts of the central pier would indicate. The elongated octagonal form, requiring an unusual pattern in the vaults, was probably decided by the closeness of the chapter house to the outer north wall of the choir. Chapter house and vestibule were built in the 1240s.

Right at the east end stands the Lady chapel whose brilliantly coloured glass has, in fact, offered an anticipation of pleasure in glimpses right from the first entrance. It is an aisleless church built by William Eyton between 1320 and 1336, exquisite in design both inside and out, with its steeply pointed windows now filled with glass of the early sixteenth century bought in 1802 from the abbey of Herckenrode in what is now Belgium. Originally intended to stand separate from the choir, this Lady chapel is out of alignment from the main body of the cathedral and so, when William Ramsey was asked to join choir and Lady chapel together after the latter's completion, he rebuilt the presbytery, making the connexion as unobtrusive as possible by swinging the axis round from one bay to the next, giving a wholly pleasurable effect.

right above: **Looking through Gilbert Scott's screen to the high altar and the Lady chapel**

right below: **The chapter house showing the central pier**

A monk's head in the chapter house

Lincoln

IF DURHAM is the greatest Romanesque cathedral, then Lincoln is probably the greatest Gothic cathedral of all those considered in this book, whether judged from its position, originality and brilliance in its grand conceptions, or the wealth of its decorative features and furnishings. It is possible to spend days merely on the sculpture and details of its exterior without ever going inside to see the equally extensive riches of its interior. More than any other cathedral it conveys the sense of a special mission handed on from one generation of architects and sculptors to another – the celebration of life through the art of praise, apparent in work of all periods, in abundant foliage, jutting crockets, the patent eroticism of certain carvings and the delight in all the varieties of physiognomy and temperament in human nature.

The west front showing the Norman portals set in the thirteenth-century arcaded screen

The see was removed here from Dorchester-on-Thames in Oxfordshire in 1073 by the Norman bishop, Remigius, who built the first cathedral; part of his work remains in the west front. The usual fires led to further building under Bishop Alexander, but an even greater disaster occurred on 15 April 1185. There was an earthquake in which most of the cathedral was reduced to ruin or to an unsafe condition. The next year a man who was to be regarded as one of the greatest saints of medieval England was made bishop, Hugh of Avalon, a Carthusian monk from near Grenoble, torn from his seclusion by his ecclesiastical superiors and known later as Great St Hugh to distinguish him from the boy saint of Lincoln, Little St Hugh, whose cult as the pretended victim of ritual murder by the Jews of Lincoln is one of the nastier aspects of the city's history. Great St Hugh began the rebuilding with the choir and eastern transepts which were constructed under the direction of Geoffrey de Noyers and Richard Mason between 1192 and 1210. This was followed shortly in the period 1215–55 by the building of the great transept, the chapter house, the nave, the extension of the west front, the Galilee and the lower part of the central tower, all, except the great transept, under an architect called Alexander. Much of this work was carried out in the episcopate (1235–53) of another great bishop, Robert Grosseteste, a formidable intellectual and one of the founders of Western experimental science. With the building of the Angel Choir between 1256 and 1280 for the remains of St Hugh by the Yorkshireman, Simon of Thirsk, Lincoln entered a new architectural age with one of the master works of the early Decorated style. In the early fourteenth century the cloisters were added and the central tower was completed, and by the end of the century the cathedral had its spired west towers and a wealth of carved stone and woodwork in its interior.

Its profile of three towers majestically complements the high limestone

top: **Detail of a Romanesque jamb shaft in the central doorway of the west front** *and below* **Victorian recutting in a jamb shaft of the west front: compare this with the original**

far left: **One of the series of kings over the central doorway of the west front**

The Galilee porch protruding from the south transept

The Judgement portal, flanked by Perpendicular chapels, that leads into the Angel Choir

right: The carving that gives the Judgement portal its name: Christ on the Last Day, surrounded by angels; Hell's mouth with its demons is below His feet

The east front with the central tower beyond *(right)*

ridge on which it rides, visible for miles in many directions over the flatter Lincolnshire countryside. The central tower, now 271 feet high, once carried a spire of lead-encased timber said to have reached the almost unbelievable height of 525 feet. The spire fell down in 1548 and should, of course, be replaced, as should those of the west towers removed in 1807. It would, for once, provide a worthy use for the techniques and knowledge of today and at the same time would restore an essential element of the Gothic to the cathedral, the God-seeking urge of the spire which its makers intended it should express.

To walk around the exterior is an extraordinary and exciting experience; the whole building is so complex and so rich in detail that we zigzag backwards and forwards trying to marry the design of the great parts to the intriguing profusion of human heads, demons and angels that round every corner invite inspection. This is true not only of the west front with its thirteenth-century arcaded screen encasing the early Norman incuttings for the doors, decorated with some of the finest Romanesque sculpture in the country, but also of the whole length of the south side with its alternation of wide and thin buttresses, the looping out of the Galilee porch, the shadowed yard made between the two transepts and the exceptional beauty of the surviving carving of the south-east porch with the nearby statues presumed to be of Edward I and his second wife, Margaret of Valois. This is a Judgement portal with Christ censed by angels appearing to rule over scenes of resurrection, of souls raised to bliss or dragged to hell by demons, while kings, queens, angels and wise and foolish virgins soar in the orders overhead, and the battered figures of the Old and the New Law, Synagogue and Ecclesia, face one another in the side walls as though from the ultimate reaches of time. Here too there is much rich foliage and birds peck at berries or perch quite unconcerned at the end of the world. This porch concentrates the spirit of

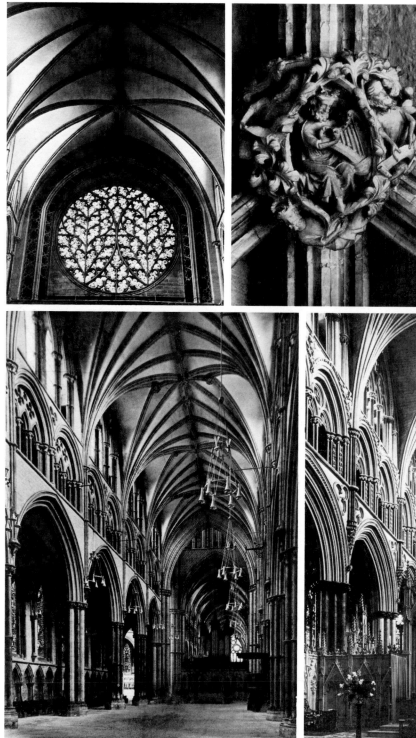

far left: The 'Bishop's Eye', the Decorated rose window in the south transept

left: David playing the harp: a boss in the south choir aisle

below left: The nave looking east

below right: The high altar with its eighteenth-century Gothick canopy and the Angel Choir beyond

Head of a negro in the Angel Choir

Figures in the triforium spandrels of the Angel Choir:
left: Angel with a scroll
right: Virgin and Child with a censing angel

Lincoln, where the sublime and the trivial are contained and made to accord in a capacious harmony. All along this great south side of the cathedral, time and again the aesthetic assault arouses forgotten memories and unnamed emotions so intense that the only relief is to look at the windows of the central tower for calm and reassurance. Turning round the east front, we find that the same aesthetic assault begins again on the north side with its variety of the flying buttresses of the decagonal chapter house, the connexion of the cloister with the two north transepts and the tremendous certainty of the tower.

It is almost a relief to enter the nave which is so pure, so abstract, with its Purbeck shafts and the subtle double arcading along the aisle walls. Once in the transepts the assault begins again with the more sober Dean's Eye, the rose window of the north transept, gazing at the Bishop's Eye, an insertion of the Decorated period made of a design of two leaves side by side. Of the same period is the pulpitum, a feast of foliage. This is bordered by arched gateways into the choir aisles with men in ritual combat with monsters in the capitals from which rise sprays of deeply undercut leafage. The choir itself, with its stalls that have no equal except those of Chester and its strange crazy vaulting, with ribs interloping across the bays, maintains the force of multitudinous impressions, only assuaged a little by the furnishings around the high altar, the soldiers asleep under the Easter sepulchre and the great tomb of Chaucer's sister-in-law, Katherine Swinford, mistress and wife to John of Gaunt. The aisles alongside the choir are beset with faces and figures on the walls and in the bosses of the vaults, wimpled ladies, fierce clerics, wrestlers and knights. And then we come upon the Angel Choir, named after the smiling and wide-winged beings in the spandrels of the triforium arches, where the great traceried window almost completely takes up the central wall of the east end, allowing light to pour into what is one of the noblest interiors of the Middle Ages. Much of the sculpture in the triforium - not only the angels, but also the heads of pagans, a negro, women, bishops and saints – is of a quality to match their setting. But it is the impression of the whole that makes this the artistic culmination of Lincoln – a place where the riot of aesthetic sensations, alternatively aroused and temporarily satisfied by what we have already seen, is changed into a radiant consummation of peace.

Norwich

THE FIRST OF THE EAST ANGLIAN CATHEDRALS was founded at Dunwich in AD 630, but long ago tumbled over a cliff into the sea. In about AD 670 the see was divided between Dunwich and North Elmham where there are remains of the Saxon cathedral. For a short time after the Conquest the see was transferred to Thetford, but this caused such quarrels between the bishop and the abbot of Bury St Edmunds that in 1094 it was moved to Norwich, an important town and conveniently distant from the abbot. The bishop responsible for the move and for building the cathedral was Herbert de Losinga who had bought his bishopric from William Rufus, a practice known as simony and one particularly condemned by the Reformers of the time. There was an outcry from the monks who soon convinced de Losinga of his sin and he built the cathedral as an act of expiation after a journey to Rome to obtain absolution. He also brought in monks from Canterbury to found the new monastery to be attached to the cathedral.

The building of the cathedral began in 1096 with the apsidal east end. Here was brought the old bishop's cathedra of stone, probably originally from North Elmham, to stand in the traditional position of early Christianity behind the high altar. Though much restored, the throne in its setting is one of the few examples in northern Europe of this early plan that is still in use. Herbert de Losinga urged on the building of the cathedral as well as the quarters for the monks and by his death in 1119 work had probably begun on the nave. The main body of the cathedral was completed under his two successors, Eborard, who completed the nave, and William de Turbe, who built the tower. The main additions of later periods included all the high vaulting and the great fifteenth-century spire which rises from the Norman tower, but they adorned rather than hid or replaced the twelfth-century work.

It must have been extremely well built to withstand all the fires that devastated it. The wooden roof of the nave was burnt in about 1170. A hundred years later, in 1272, a bitter quarrel broke out between the prior and the townsmen about the prior's rights to impose tolls on a local fair; the prior armed his monks and, reinforced with mercenaries, led a pillaging attack on the city. The outraged men of Norwich in return slung burning missiles into the monastery and on to the cathedral roof; everything went up in flames and apart from the recently vaulted Lady chapel the buildings were roofless. Terrible retribution was visited on the ringleaders and the city had to pay heavily for the damage. Then, in 1463, the timber spire on the central tower was struck by lightning and once more the nave roof went up in the ensuing fire. It was after this that the cathedral received its high vaulting and the stone spire.

The Norman tower with its fifteenth-century spire

The Norman nave with its fifteenth-century vaulting

Vaulting bosses of the nave showing (a) the sequence of the Passion (b) the opening through which a censer was lowered

The interior of the nave presents a marriage of the earliest and the latest styles of architecture of our period, and a far happier marriage of Norman frame with Gothic vaults than, for example, may be seen in the nave of Gloucester. Here there is none of the disproportion of the tremendous drums of Gloucester: the triforium is allowed its full place in the design, rising to the same height as the arcades beneath and with spacious openings that allow deep diagonal views of the shafting on the inner sides repeating the pattern set below. Traces of the painting that must have survived the fire of 1272 remain in one bay, but of the rest all is gone. The stone carving is very simple with cushion capitals to the shafts; this probably means that the finer decorative detail was all carried out by painters. The interior is also now far better lit by the big west window introduced to show up the stone vaulting than ever could have been the intention, or indeed within the capacity, of the

View from the choir showing
the Norman apse surmounted
by the Perpendicular clerestory
and vaulting

original designers. Of the vault of the nave we will say more later. One
interesting feature of Norwich is that it preserves the arrangement common
to monastic cathedrals whereby the monks' choir extended under the
crossing and into the first bays of the nave. In Worcester, for example, after
the Reformation the choir stalls were moved eastward beyond the crossing.
Past the organ loft we come upon one of the great sights of England – the
rounded Norman apse about the high altar, with the throne beyond it and,
rising above the triforium, a sudden flowering of Gothic in the clerestory

windows of about 1360, surmounted by Bishop Goldwell's vaulting of about 1480. These Gothic additions are like an aisleless Lady chapel that has taken to flight. The glass of about 1840 is good enough to support the general impression of levitation which is increased by the way the vaults spring from ogee arches, each formed from shafts detached from the thin wall divisions between the windows. There are 132 bosses. From the massive ambulatory about the presbytery extend numerous chapels of different dates, including the modern St Saviour's chapel, built in the 1930s where the Lady chapel, ruined in Elizabethan times once stood. Among the furnishings of these chapels are many examples of altarpieces by the Norwich school of painters, known as retables. In the vault of the nave the 225 bosses there set out to tell a story – no less than the history of creation from the first day to the Last Judgement – in bold carvings so arranged that the Old Testament subjects starting from the crossing prefigure the events of the New Testament that begin in the eighth bay. In the tenth bay the pattern is interrupted by a hole through which, it is thought, the figure of an angel was suspended at Whitsuntide, and which was also used to let down a censer which would be swung above the heads of the people, letting out clouds of incense in rhythmic oscillations – a similar practice is still observed at Santiago de Compostela in Spain.

The cloisters, built between 1297 and 1430, exhibit a similar wealth in the carvings of the bosses with themes from Revelations in the south and west walks and scenes from the life of Christ in the north and part of the east walks. All this is only a part of what must have been lost, because Norwich with its fifty-six parish churches of medieval times was a great centre of crafts associated with the cults of religion, of workers in alabaster, painters of retables and glaziers, all trades largely wiped out by the Reformation.

below centre and right: **Two scenes from the sequence of bosses in the cloisters depicting the Apocalypse: Babylon and an angel with the trumpet and the rivers of blood**

below: **Cloister walk**

Oxford

WHEN OXFORD was first created as a separate see in 1542, the church chosen as the cathedral was that of Oseney Abbey, a building of exceptional grandeur and now utterly destroyed. Unfortunately, four years later the see was removed to the church of St Frideswide which had been engulfed by the new college founded by Cardinal Wolsey and taken over by Henry VIII as Christ Church. St Frideswide was a nun who suffered from the attentions of a Saxon chieftain who was struck blind when he set out to rape her. Her shrine was guarded by a community of nuns until 1049 when the foundation was changed first to that of secular canons (until 1111) and then to the Augustinians (until 1524).

It is now the smallest of English cathedrals, because it lost half of its Norman nave when the enormous and never completed Tom Quad was built between 1525 and 1529 for the new college. It is almost completely masked by the quadrangle except for its pure thirteenth-century spire that rises with a kind of reproach above the evidence of later luxury and ostentation. Its only entrance is through the quadrangle, much of which acts as a close for the dignitaries of the cathedral which is also the college chapel.

The loss of so much of the nave means that the visitor is impelled almost

left: **Vaulting of the choir** *and right:* **one of the pendants of the choir vaulting**

The choir showing the recessed triforium stage of the Norman work, the vaulting begun in 1478 and Gilbert Scott's Romanesque revival east wall

The north transept looking towards the Latin chapel

immediately into the choir, an interior which presents a marriage of Norman and late Gothic like Norwich, but with very different elements and effects. It is different not only because of the smaller scale but because of the curious way in which the triforium stage is treated. In this late Norman work (roughly dated 1158–80) the triforium is tucked under the arches of the nave arcade and recessed. The effect is odd, but nothing to dwell on, as the eye is caught by the splendid vaulting begun in 1478 with its fans that spring from pendants, themselves carried by arches that rise from the bottom of the clerestory. Ribs like icing form a pattern of crowns down the centres of the vaults – an exquisite and charming creation. The east end is an essay in the Norman style by Gilbert Scott who carried out much restoration and new work here in the last century. There remains some good fourteenth-century glass in the south aisle and in the Latin chapel. The cloisters were also amputated by the building of the college, and off them lies the thirteenth-century chapter house.

Peterborough

THE MONASTERY AT PETERBOROUGH was founded on the edge of the fenlands in AD 654 or AD 655 by the royal family of Mercia on their conversion to Christianity. This first monastery was attacked by the Norsemen in AD 870 who murdered the monks including the abbot, Hedda, and destroyed the settlement. A carved stone, now behind the high altar, was traditionally considered to be their memorial. It is, in fact, even earlier in date, about AD 800. The monastery was rebuilt about AD 965, and the remains of the Saxon minster were uncovered during work in the last century. This church survived the sack of the monastery in 1070 by Hereward the Wake only to be burned in a fire in 1116 started by a servant, it is said, who, having trouble in kindling some wood, invoked the devil's aid. The devil willingly obliged. As a result we have in Peterborough one of the grandest of all Norman abbey churches, all the more important because it retains its original rounded apse. The apse, chancel, transepts and part of the south wall of the nave were built between 1118 and 1150. The nave was largely completed by 1175, but the original intentions for the west front in which towers would have risen over the ninth bays from the east of the nave were never carried out. First the nave was extended, then the western transepts with towers were constructed, and finally the extraordinary screen front, with its three deep niches, the gables over them and the turrets at the sides, was built to make one of the most astonishing of all early Gothic exteriors.

Of later work the Lady chapel built about 1290, like that of Ely in the northeast angle of transept and chancel, and an octagon over the modified Norman central tower, again an influence from Ely, no longer survive. Under Abbot Kirkton (1496–1528) the very beautiful retrochoir with its fan vaulting was built. Two unhappy queens were buried here; the divorced Catharine of Aragon in 1536 and the decapitated Mary, Queen of Scots, in 1587. Mary's body was removed on the command of her son, James VI and I, to Westminster Abbey. The exterior view of the apse, rising above the tall statues on the buttresses of the retrochoir, with spired turrets at the start of the hemicircle, is particularly impressive. Strange faces stare out of the roundels in the parapet above the Norman arcades and the later Decorated tracery of the windows, inserted to give more light to the high altar and the chancel. Inside, the chancel, which terminates in the apse, is high and ample, drawing the eye right from the first entrance at the west end because there is no screen or pulpitum to interrupt the view. The original ceiling was replaced in the fifteenth century with the present intricately carved wooden ceiling. There is much variety in the Norman design; the piers are octagonal, round and twelve-sided and the tympana in the triforium stage are all differently

The three arches with their gables of the west front

The Norman south transept with the central tower

ornamented. The exterior fronts of the transepts are both stratified with arcading and provide admirable examples of how the Norman architects tried to lighten the heaviness of their compositions by breaking up big wall spaces with small members.

The nave is long, high and grand. As at Norwich, the insertion of later windows to the gallery of the triforium stage effectively increases the intake of light. One of its most remarkable features is its wooden roof of about 1220 painted with lozenges, intricately bordered and containing an odd variety of figures within their borders, monsters, musicians, an architect, a Janus head amongst the more conventional kings, queens and holy men. The effect is that of embroidery or eastern weaving as though it were the richly decorated canopy of a tent. At its western end the nave broadens out into transepts with pointed arches announcing the transition into the screen of the west front.

This screen is very strange; it consists of three immense arches forming a loggia for the three west doors of the abbey. Where one would expect the central arch to be wider than those on either side, to give suitable importance to the main entrance, it is in fact narrower. The side doors, having to lead into the aisles of the nave, are not centred within their arches. Spired turrets stand at either end of the screen and there are spirelets between the gables. On the northern side rears one of the transept towers, its corner pinnacles protruding above the gable; this tower has lost its spire, while the companion tower and spire on the south side was never completed. It may even be that a greater, higher spire on the old central tower was intended to dominate the whole so that the present lesser collection of spires would seem like successive statements of a theme only fully developed in this central spire and so also that the arches of the screen would be topped by a superstructure in receding planes that would balance their giant scale. That this was never completed is

left: **The fan-vaulted retrochoir**

Pierced arch and fan vaulting where the retrochoir adjoins the Norman apse

View across the nave

The Norman nave with its painted roof and the uninterrupted view to the apsidal sanctuary

one matter for regret; another is that in the later fourteenth century a porch was inserted in the centre opening, thereby blocking the free passage and open nature of the loggia behind the arches. This west front arouses strong feelings: some detest it; others regard it as one of the supreme masterworks of the Gothic in England. It has been shown that the proportions of the scheme are based on the double square, with ratios of width and height of arches and corner towers that correspond to the proportions in classical music of diapason (the octave), diapente (the fifth) and diatesseron (the fourth). The impression of the whole, ruled by the rising shafts of the arches grouped in sixes, recalls ancient legends of Merlin and of pagan mythology when stone was made to pile on stone by the power of voice and instrument alone.

Ripon

A NOTICE IN THE WEST ENTRANCE of Ripon advises the use of the south porch in the cathedral in windy weather, a detail that emphasizes at once the exposed site the cathedral occupies and the courtesy extended to the visitor in this ancient town. St Cuthbert himself was once guestmaster in the first Christian foundation on the site, that of Celtic monks in the seventh century, and here he once unawares entertained an angel. It was a cathedral for a short time in the period of St Wilfrid, who is generally thought to have built the crypt here. After various vicissitudes it became a collegiate church with secular canons tied to the archbishopric of York. In 1836 it was made the see of a new diocese.

The cathedral is built on an east-facing ridge above the confluence of the rivers Ure and Skell. Approached from the town, the west front presents a composition of exceptional elegance with two flanking towers and stages of lancet windows rising above the triple portals. The towers have lost their long thin spires, but in other ways, since Gilbert Scott removed some later Decorated tracery in the lancets, it must present much of its original appearance. The interior of the nave has many curiosities; the original nave built in about 1180 was without aisles and apparently lit only from the clerestory level. Some very interesting work of this period remains at the west end of the nave which is otherwise late Perpendicular work by Christopher

Samson bearing off the gates of
Gaza: detail of a misericord

View from the choir, showing the forceful tracery of the east window

The Early English west front

Scune between 1502 and 1522. He constructed the aisles and the bays of the nave, but was never able to finish the crossing, which explains its present very odd appearance. An entrance just before the crossing leads down to the Saxon crypt. It has a sequence of underground rooms with niches in the stone for wall-lights and the way through leads up again into the choir. Here there is a great mingling of periods, the east end dominated by a late thirteenth-century window and the two west bays on the south, like the pulpitum, rebuilt in about 1480 when the central tower collapsed. It is a fine, well-lit interior and one of the chief pleasures is in the choir stalls with their spired tabernacle work, their misericords and the zoo of mythical animals in the carvings. As a boy, Lewis Carroll knew these carvings well and it would not be surprising if they influenced the making of the Alice books. A wooden hand, worked by a pedal from the organ loft, projects above the entrance to the choir, to beat time for the choristers. From the south aisle of the choir we enter the chapter house, a Norman room with singular round windows like great eyes. Above it is the former Lady chapel which now houses the library.

Rochester

IN MANY OF THE MORE DISTANT VIEWS, especially from the river Medway, the cathedral at Rochester is inseparable from the great twelfth-century keep of the castle which tends to overshadow it. Nevertheless, the cathedral, though possessing individual features of greater interest than its overall impression, has an important history. Founded in AD 604, the second English diocese in date after Canterbury, it numbers among its bishops Paulinus, the apostle of Northumbria and founder of York, and St John Fisher, beheaded like his friend, Thomas More, by Henry VIII for refusing the oath of supremacy. Another notable holder of the see was Gundulf of Bec, the first Norman bishop here and chief castle builder to William the Conqueror. He built the White Tower of London and parts of Dover and Rochester castles. When he came to replace the Saxon cathedral, true to his training, his first aim was to build an immensely strong tower, both as a belfry and as a treasury. Of eleventh-century work only the lower parts of this tower and part of the crypt are still visible.

The cathedral is largely twelfth-century, including the broad nave and the

The west front   The west door   Westward view of the nave

restored west front. The west door, much weathered and recut, is one of the chief examples of Romanesque sculpture in England. The elaborate voussoirs contain carvings of leaves and of beasts sinking their teeth into their backs or tails, strange examples of mortification to set against the tympanum with its battered figure of Christ in Majesty, surrounded by angels and emblems of the Evangelists and with the apostles on the lintel. Two figures, Solomon and the Queen of Sheba, grow out of jamb shafts on either side of the door; they are column figures, a style first devised at St Denis in France and rarely copied in this country.

Fourteenth-century wall painting of the Wheel of Fortune

A prophet in the chapter house doorway   **The Early English presbytery**

In 1201 a Scots pilgrim on his way to the Holy Land was murdered outside Rochester; as miracles were associated with him, he became known as St William of Perth and his shrine attracted many visitors and much wealth. In this period, from the proceeds of this new income, the present presbytery, the eastern transepts and the choir were built, while the transepts were reconstructed. The presbytery is unusual for a cathedral in being aisleless and in having only two stages instead of the customary three. The present choir stalls incorporate parts of early thirteenth-century ones and are the earliest examples to survive in England. Of later work, a lovely decorated door into what is now the chapter house and the very late Perpendicular Lady chapel were significant additions. The chapter house doorway of about 1340 has a marvellously crocketed ogee outer arch which contains an inner band of figures, Ecclesia and the blindfold Synagogue on either side and above them a panoply of prophets or doctors of the Church. The cathedral underwent three very heavy restorations in the last century.

St Albans

As ST ALBAN was the first native of these islands to be martyred for the Christian faith, the monastery that grew round his shrine came to be one of the greatest centres of pilgrimage and one of the most richly endowed of all foundations. The enormous abbey church, the second largest in England after Winchester, bears witness to this wealth; unfortunately, it was not raised to cathedral status under Henry VIII which might have led to a fuller preservation of the fabric of the church as well as of the monastic buildings. It was only raised to cathedral status in 1877. At the time of this event, an amateur architect, Lord Grimthorpe, paying for the restoration himself, was then allowed a completely free hand to do whatsoever he liked – and what he liked has met with resounding disapproval ever since.

St Alban was a citizen of the Roman town of Verulam, whose ruins lie close to the cathedral. Though a pagan, he gave shelter and help to a Christian deacon, Amphibalus, in flight from the Diocletian persecution of AD 303–5. They were both caught and executed: St Alban, having become a Christian,

The reredos of the high altar with doors leading to the shrines in the retrochoir beyond: the sculptures are all Victorian replacements; the roofing is thirteenth-century woodwork

The nave, tower and south transept seen from the south-west

refused to sacrifice at a pagan altar and was condemned to death. The place of execution was the site now occupied by the north transept. So many people crammed the bridge over the river leading to this place that St Alban went down to the bank and the waters parted for him and his party. The appointed executioner refused to carry out his task. At the top of the hill Alban asked for water and a spring burst forth at his feet. A soldier took the place of the executioner and, when he cut off Alban's head, the soldier's eyes fell to the ground. The reluctant executioner was then beheaded. The cult of St Alban was strong amongst the Roman Christians and the rediscovery of his relics and those of St Amphibalus in the time of King Offa was authenticated by a surviving account of the sixth century. Offa founded a Benedictine monastery here in AD 793, another act of atonement for the murder of Ethelbert for which he also endowed Hereford.

The church was completely rebuilt under the first two Norman abbots, Paul of Caen (1077–93) and Richard d'Albini (1097–1119). The long period between their rules was because William Rufus, by not appointing an abbot, could keep the revenues to himself. The monks were obviously very proud of their architect, Robert Mason, because the chronicle of the abbey praises him above all his contemporaries. Saxon abbots had already been collecting Roman tiles from the ruins of Verulam with the purpose of rebuilding and Robert drew on this store in the building of the great tower – a magnificent creation with its warm and varied colours, setting off, by its height, the vast length of the church. The finest surviving part of his work in the interior is the crossing and the choir which extends three bays westward into the nave. The nave itself beyond the rood screen is a strange jumble; there are Norman piers on the north side but many of those facing them fell down in 1323 and were replaced in much the same style as the thirteenth-century work which had extended the nave to the west front. Lord Grimthorpe was responsible for the

Baluster shafts in the triforium of the north transept

left: Wall paintings on Norman piers of the nave. Formerly altars stood against these piers

Roman bricks used with flint in the exterior of the south transept

The base of the shrine of St Alban

present awesomely hideous appearance of the west front and for remodelling the north transept. There are, however, two distinctive features to the nave: one is the series of wall paintings on the lateral sides of the Norman piers set there for a series of altars in the bays; the other is the stone roodscreen, perhaps the work of Henry Yeveley, the only surviving one of its kind, cutting the choir from the nave. A similar division is made between the choir and the chapel of St Alban by an important fifteenth-century stone reredos, whose niches are now filled with rather good late Victorian statues (not the work of Lord Grimthorpe). Doors on either side of the reredos lead into the shrine of the saint. The reconstituted base of the shrine, put together from 2,000 fragments found in 1872, but originally richly carved after 1302, is the dramatic focus of this remarkable space. To one side is the wooden watching loft where a monk always kept guard over the jewels and gold of the shrine and on the other is the tomb of Duke Humphrey of Gloucester, brother of Henry V and guardian of the young Henry VI, with a late thirteenth-century ironwork grille separating it from the aisle. The body of the saint and the watching monks have all long ago vanished, but a deep memory is preserved here, of heroism and wakeful fortitude, safe against time and the vicissitudes of religious conflict. Beyond this shrine extends the fourteenth-century Lady chapel.

St Albans is also remarkable for the amount of medieval wall paintings that survive there. It must be remembered that it harboured one of the most influential schools of illumination in the country and that one of its artists, the monk Matthew Paris, was one of the greatest historians of the Middle Ages. Some of these paintings, especially the thirteenth-century crucifixions and other subjects on the nave piers, are remarkable works of art. The most moving, though, is later in date: this is the depiction of doubting Thomas, inserting his hand into the wound in Christ's side. Christ grasps Thomas's hand by the wrist to guide it more surely into the gash made by the lance and from his mouth come the words, 'Blessed are they that have not seen and yet have believed.' To which Thomas says, 'My Lord and my God.'

Salisbury

The west front

ON THE ROAD NORTH of Salisbury one passes a great mound of earthworks that looks like one of the many iron-age fortresses of Wiltshire. It is, in fact, the town of Old Sarum, a Norman town with castle and cathedral that failed. The diocese of the area originally at Sherborne, then divided between Sherborne and Ramsbury, was moved to this site in 1075. Such quarrels broke out between the castle and the cathedral that in 1228, with papal permission, the see was removed south to the river Avon to the new town of Salisbury. This late beginning meant that Salisbury was built wholly in the Gothic period with no earlier building to influence its form or with portions to be incorporated in its fabric.

A great opportunity was offered and largely seized. The bishop, Richard Poore, was a man of exceptional administrative ability and among his canons was Elias of Dereham who was employed on many of the important artistic ventures of the day, either as an informed adviser or as an actual designer. Elias obviously worked very closely with the architect of Salisbury, Nicholas of Ely. The first foundation stones were laid at a ceremony in 1220 when the

below right: **The north transept**

The nave looking towards the crossing and the chancel

bishop laid stones on behalf of the pope and the legate and nobles of the neighbourhood, including the Earl and Countess of Salisbury who had contributed to the construction, also laid stones. The Lady chapel was completed in five years and the whole complex apart from the west front and the spire of the next century was finished in thirty-eight years. The town attracted scholars and foundations of learning. Salisbury rapidly develped as a centre for music and an influence in setting new liturgical standards and styles. The musical tradition survived the Reformation so that George Herbert, the seventeenth-century poet and vicar of the nearby parish of Bemerton, would go to the cathedral twice a week and at his return would say that 'his time spent in prayer and cathedral music elevated his soul and was his heaven upon earth'. To read the surviving manuals describing the rites of Sarum is to become aware of the cathedral as a theatre in continuous use throughout the Church's year, with important variations in the choice of vestments, in the routes of processions, in the singing of special sequences and anthems, with every aspect recorded as though it were the notation of a sacred choreography.

Few interiors depend so much on the weather as Salisbury's: on a fine day it can seem radiant and spacious; in dull weather it appears bare and severe – a sparseness accentuated by the loss of much of the glass in the eighteenth

In the cloister

above left: **View into the chapter house from the vestibule, showing the central pier and some of the stalls**

Three faces with four eyes, a
carving in the chapter house

Salisbury spire reflected in
the river

century when James Wyatt, in the course of improvements (which included
the destruction of two chantry chapels and a great detached belfry) had it
thrown out. There is also a lack of decorative sculpture, except for the
remarkable corbels so high up that one needs field glasses to see them. In a
way, its fame as a liturgical centre gives the clue to this severity. What we see
is the bones of a theatrical setting for dramas that are no longer performed.
The visitor will normally see it populated by other visitors; if he attends an
important service, he will get a very different impression. Other cathedrals
are changed by the presence of a large congregation; Salisbury is totally
transformed. Then the point of the open vistas becomes plain and Nicholas of
Ely's design, not as governed by the pedantic requirements of Elias of
Dereham but as the provision of a stage for clergy and people, is understood.
Nevertheless, without people, liturgy and music the architectural impression is cold, even if elegant, with extensive use of Purbeck shafts in the
columns and triforium of the nave, and throughout the transepts, choir and
Lady chapel. There is one feature, though, of supreme architectonic beauty
and that is in the relation of the eastern transepts to the choir. There is
another reminiscence of the theatre in the sequence of sixty corbel heads
found everywhere in the cathedral at the triforium level except in the Lady
chapel. Many of them are of exceptional quality and they were obviously
planned as part of a single scheme. They are so realistic that contemporary
notables have been suggested for their subjects. This would accord with the
new skill in portraiture and the new interest in individual character exhibited
by the Gothic masters of the late twelfth and early thirteenth century. Thus,
Henry III may appear amongst them twice, first as a young king and then
later in life accompanied by his sons. Bishops, noblemen and ladies are
among those represented; but these roles in life are also shown as diversities
of human temperament with supreme psychological skill. Up above our
heads a play is being enacted and it echoes the constant manoeuvring of
selves within our own personalities.

   If the interior may disappoint, the outside fulfils all hopes and imaginings of
those who come to Salisbury for the first time. Richard Mason was
responsible for the west front, now sadly filled with Victorian figures, the
cloisters and the chapter house. The cloisters, built between 1263 and 1284 in
the Geometric phase of the Decorated style, are the grandest and most
beautiful in England, with their magnificent tracery of six-lobed foils
wheeling above twin arches inviting one into the lawn with its cedars. The
chapter house, one of the finest of its kind, still retains a cycle of highly
enjoyable sculpture. The progression of the south and west aisles of the
cloisters grants fuller and fuller views of the cathedral and above all of the
spire. Built with its tower between 1320 and 1380 by Robert Mason and
Richard Farleigh, this is the highest and the noblest spire of its period in the
world. It rises to 404 feet with a stirring combination of strength and ecstatic
striving; it dominates the city and all approaches for miles. Its tower alone,
with its tall lights surging upwards, would have been remarkable had only
that ever been completed, but the masons did more. They announced the
theme of the spire in lesser steeples at the corners and in the wall centres,
made higher pointed pinnacles sprout behind them and then laid their claim
to heaven in the great banded spire itself.

Southwark

ONLY MADE A SEE in 1905, Southwark was formerly known as St Mary Overie, Overie meaning 'over the water of the Thames'. It was particularly associated with the bishops of Winchester who owned a palace nearby, a liberty (or area of private jurisdiction) known as the Clink, with a prison that has given its name wider currency, and numerous houses of ill-fame from which much of the bishops' wealth was derived. The church's history as a foundation goes back to Saxon times and in 1106 it became a house of the Augustinian regular canons. The present nave is almost wholly the work of Sir Arthur Blomfield between 1890 and 1897 in which he copied the thirteenth-century chancel. The chancel and the retrochoir were built after a fire in 1212. The retrochoir, one of the finest medieval interiors to survive in London, consists of four parallel aisles of the same height, providing with its simple piers a sober, but spacious, effect. The chancel seems to show in certain details such as the design of the triforium a strong influence from contemporary work in France. This is also to be seen in the disposition of the vaulting shafts and in the quadripartite vaulting itself. A dominant feature of the chancel is the much restored reredos of about 1520. The transepts are later thirteenth-century, though the south transept was altered in about 1440. Henry Yeveley may have built the lower stage of the tower, which was completed by Thomas Berty at the same time as he did the reredos. The cathedral holds the tombs of John Gower, Chaucer's friend and fellow poet, and of Lancelot Andrewes, the most learned and perhaps the holiest man ever to hold the see of Winchester, who translated part of the Authorized Version of the Bible. Shakespeare, whose Globe Theatre stood nearby, must have known this church well, as did John Harvard, the founder of Harvard University, who is commemorated here in a chapel named after him off the north transept.

The crossing and choir showing the reredos

The retrochoir

Southwell

SOUTHWELL is chiefly, and justly, famous for the leaf carvings of its chapter house. Even without them it would be remarkable, both in its other architectural features, its environment and its history. In the mid tenth century the manor was granted to Archbishop Oskatel of York. A college of secular canons was founded there and successive archbishops of York were particularly attached to their palace, the remains of which stand beside the present cathedral. The college of canons wielded considerable power, both ecclesiastical and temporal, over the surrounding country and from their minster they exercised many of the functions of a cathedral chapter. The Norman church, begun in 1108 under Archbishop Thomas of York, was unusual for its time in possessing a square-ended chancel; this was replaced in the thirteenth century but, apart from that, the main body of the church is all Romanesque – towers, transepts and nave. By good fortune, the chapter survived the Reformation and to the comfortable livings afforded generations of canons are owed the many handsome old houses that stand close to the minster. The chapter was dissolved in 1840, and in 1884 Southwell was made a bishopric with Nottinghamshire as its diocese.

The Norman nave

Exterior showing the spired west towers and front and the central tower

Right: The chancel side of the pulpitum

Buttercups on a capital on the right of the portal

Because it retains its spired west towers (the spires were replaced in 1880) and because every part west of the chancel is basically Norman, Southwell is one of the best preserved examples of a Romanesque church. Both inside and out the Norman portions have many features of interest, the porthole-like windows of the clerestory, the wide arches of the triforium which never received the inner divisions they were intended to have, the gables of the transepts completely filled with zigzags and circle decoration, the west front with those two elegant towers (the big west window is fifteenth-century) and the mouldings of the central tower. It is a bold, plain and jolly church – that is until you reach the luscious decoration of the pulpitum, a brilliant example of its kind, through which the Early English choir and chancel, begun in 1234 under Archbishop Walter de Grey, is reached. This is far subtler work, original insofar as the triforium stage is abolished for the deepening of the tall lancets of the clerestory and having a vitality in its lines that makes the Norman style it superseded puddingy and dumpy by comparison. The good humour survives, but here it is refined into a beneficent and spacious mood that is a splendid preparation for the chief joy of Southwell, the chapter house, reached by a vestibule from the north aisle of the chancel.

The chapter house must have been built about 1290. Nothing is known about the genius who designed it and carved, or had carved to his direction, the foliage, flowers and figures that sprout or project all about it. This decoration begins in the twin doorway in the chancel aisle, continues up a straight arcaded corridor into the vestibule where another portal arched with buttercup and vineleaves and shafted with Purbeck marble leads into the octagonal chapter house. This, like the chapter house at York, has no central pillar but, unlike York, the vaulting is of stone. From a central boss of leaves that cannot be identified with any particular plant – unlike most of the other foliage here – the ridges of the vault spread out through sixteen other bosses to swing down the shafts dividing the six windows and two blind sides of the chapter house. There are thirty-six stalls each with leafy tympana and capitals. There are forty-five of these capitals in the chapter house and forty-nine in the corridor and vestibule, and, although many particular species recur such as buttercup, vine, maple, hawthorn, ivy, hop and tormentil, each one seizes the eye as a wholly individual treatment. The idea of using precise delineations of foliage may have come from Rheims, and there are other continental examples such as at Naumburg; what is clear at Southwell is that the sculptor studied the plants in their natural state with intensity and love and got to know their habits of growth so that the very nodules on their twigs and the angles at which the leaves spring from the stalks entered his soul and were absorbed into his inner vision of the divine signature in the works of creation. These carvings, deeply undercut and with a lithe grace that stands out all the more for the shadows under their foliage, convey an extraordinary feeling; it is as though they were exercises in self-knowledge for the sculptor and, as he carved the limestone, at the same time he investigated and brought to the light of consciousness some latent bud of feeling in his heart. Their very precision and beauty have this effect of self-discovery on the visitor and under their power we recognize the world of nature within ourselves. As if to emphasize this point, he carved monsters and animals and men and women amongst the leaves and in the chapter house portal in the outer frieze of vineleaves at the point of the arch he carved a man who looks out at us from the leaves, observing and exemplifying the true fruit of Christ the vine: humanity redeemed in the recovery of Eden.

The entrance portal of the chapter house

Right: **The man in the vine at the apex of the outer arch of the portal**

Wells

WELLS IS FULL OF MYSTERIES, wonders and individual charms. Why this small, out-of-the-way town on the slopes of the Mendips should have been chosen as the site for the earliest completely Gothic cathedral in Europe – in the sense that the pointed arch was used here throughout for the first time – is a matter of unsatisfiable conjecture. In many of its most notable features, the west screen with its three hundred figures, the quality of much of the internal carving, the strainer arches of the crossing, the linked complex of choir, retrochoir and Lady chapel and the chapter house mounted high on an undercroft and approached by its river-like staircase, it never ceases, after repeated visits, to stir a sense of the marvellous. And its setting with the swans in the moat of the Bishop's Palace, the fourteenth-century street of houses for the vicars of the canons, the medieval gateways and expanses of lawn, perfectly complements both the beauty of its exterior and the feeling that the cathedral was evoked by magic out of the spirit of the countryside around it.

First created a see in AD 909, Wells then lost its bishop to Bath in 1090, and after many squabbles regained the see which since the thirteenth century has

The nave vaulting and the modern rood placed on the strainer arch

The west front with the central tower rising beyond. To the left is the bridge crossing the road to the street of the vicars choral

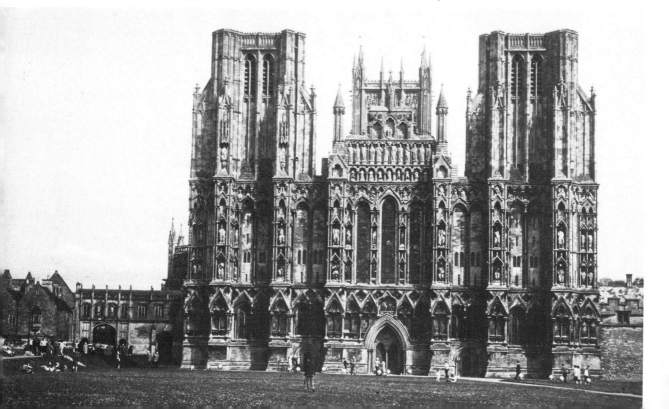

been known as that of Bath and Wells. Saxon and Norman buildings must have preceded the present cathedral on which work appears to have begun about 1176. This phase of building, lasting to about 1240, saw the construction of the choir, transepts, the nave, north porch and the west front. The chapter house was built between 1286 and 1306 and this was followed by the extension and rebuilding of the eastern parts, the completion of the central tower and the provision of the strainer arches in the course of the fourteenth century. Because of reconstruction in that period little visible remains of the chancel and choir of the late twelfth-century Gothic church which would have been the first part built. This was followed by the transepts with their double aisles and their delightful carvings – a man with toothache, a lizard feeding on berries, work in a vineyard being amongst the subjects. Both the nave, which was built next, and the transepts are now dominated, indeed overwhelmed visually, by the great strainer arches inserted after the building of the central tower. Their pattern is said to copy the saltire cross of St Andrew, to whom the cathedral is dedicated. Magnificent in their bold, masculine strength, they are hard to ignore when one is studying the nave with its totally different atmosphere. The piers are of great thickness but so richly ribbed with shafts that they are like a fine beechwood. Their capitals are probably the best examples of stiff-leaf foliage in England, growing in luxuriance as the piers approach the west end. Bare spandrels above the arches support the band of pointed arches of the triforium, and above them rises the vault, exceptional in its purity and elegance. Adam Lock, who probably built transepts and nave, is also credited with the north porch, one of the most admired features of the cathedral, a work of extraordinary intensity both inside and out. The west front and its towers is the work of another thirteenth-century master, Thomas Norreys.

This is a great screen after the model of Lincoln and Peterborough but, unlike them, with no emphasis whatsoever on the three doorways. They are so small that they have been compared to rabbit-holes in the side of a mountain. To gain width for the screen the towers were designed to stand outside the aisles of the nave. The spired towers intended by Thomas Norreys were never built and those that rise in their place are work of the late fourteenth and fifteenth centuries. The vertical impetus of the front is provided by six enormous buttresses, each carrying a complement of statues in niches

View of the nave with the strainer arch

far left: **The steps to the chapter house and the bridge**

left: **Canopied figures in buttresses of the west front**

on their inner faces as well as on their western sides. The scheme of sculpture runs in five bands all round the towers; the lowest band, 'fatally convenient for the iconoclast', has lost most of its figures except for some on the north tower which are amongst the best. Two series of quatrefoils, one with the remains of angel figures and the next with representations of Bible stories, stand beneath the tall lancets of the bays and the famous, solemn saints and wise men of Wells in their niches. Above their heads is a band of depictions of the Resurrection. The gable has three further stages; the nine angelic orders of Dionysius, the twelve apostles and finally the shattered remains of Christ on the Day of Judgement. There is no agreement on the overall iconographic scheme beyond the theme of the Resurrection though, perhaps, the current work of restoration on the front may provoke further debate. What is undeniable is the intention of the architect to astound all comers to the cathedral with the manifest depiction of the invisible world that awaited each one on death and at the end of time – an effect that would have been all the greater in the days when it glowed with gold, maroon, ultramarine and other colours and when the faces of the figures were painted to a greater semblance of life. Even without the lost adornment, it is a startling and fascinating achievement, menacing in the shadows of morning, glorious in the gold of sunset, ceremonially inviting us to consider the nature and aim of our individual souls by the presence of heroic and holy beings calling to us from the eternal world.

Whether because of lack of funds or the death of architect or designers, its towers were not completed and work came to a stop in about 1260. Twenty years later a new creative urge appeared in the chapter house. So far we have considered several of these polygonal chapter houses that approach the circle in their form. They were an English invention but their influence has been discerned as far away as the Hall of the Grand Master in the castle of the Teutonic knights at Marienburg, now in Poland. They reflect the constitutional spirit of the thirteenth century because the very disposition of the seats around their walls at equal distances from the centre affirms the equal right of those occupying them to a say in the business discussed there. The chapter house at Westminster provided the room for the House of Commons for much of its early history and at Wells, with so many Arthurian associations in the country around, we are reminded of the round table where the knights sat in similar equality. The Wells chapter house is the finest of all, with its noble central column soaring up to burst into thirty-two ribs in the vaulting, its huge windows still bearing some of the original glass, and its unique elevation on an undercroft once used as a treasury. That is the reason for the confluence of steps in the staircase leading first to the chapter house and then to a bridge built in the fifteenth century to the vicars' houses. Yet another burst of creative energy led to the building of the central tower and the Lady chapel, both designed possibly by Thomas Witney (1310–22). His Lady chapel was then joined to the choir by the building of the retrochoir by William Joy who also reconstructed the choir, providing beautiful vistas both east and west through the open arches behind the high altar. One of the loveliest parts of this later work is the east window with its dominantly gold and green glass which, suspended, above the eastward vista, seems like a hanging of translucent silk.

The central pier of the chapter house

Winchester

William Wynford's nave

WINCHESTER IS THE LONGEST CATHEDRAL IN EUROPE with a length of 556 feet. An important Roman town and, according to Mallory, the Camelot of King Arthur, the city became the capital of Wessex and was made a see in AD 662. The most famous of its Anglo-Saxon bishops was St Swithin. He had asked to be buried where passers-by should walk over him and the rain should drip from the eaves on his grave. He was, of course, far too holy to be left outside and when his body was moved into a new shrine within the old cathedral, the dead saint caused days and days of torrential downpour. That Saxon cathedral has recently been excavated. It consisted first of a small church with a separate tower; then the church was extended to include the tower.

This ancient minster was abandoned or destroyed when Walchelin, the first Norman bishop, began to build his enormous new cathedral on a different axis. It was a bold undertaking in all sorts of ways: the marshy site is fed by numerous springs – not the best site for what was to be the longest

South side of the nave seen from the ruined cloisters

cathedral in Europe – and to make the ground firm enough the builders had to drive thousands of wooden piles into the marsh before they could start the construction. The chief surviving portions of the Norman church are the crypt, the transepts and the crossing with its low tower. The crypt and transepts were built between 1079 and 1093. The first tower collapsed soon after William Rufus, killed in the New Forest in 1100 in a hunting accident or deliberately murdered, was buried at the crossing beneath it; people were not slow to find a connexion. The present tower and its adjoining bays were rebuilt between 1108 and 1120. Virtually every part of the Norman nave is now masked by the present Perpendicular nave to which we will come later. It is probable that it followed the proportions of the transepts, now seen more clearly in the north transept which is one of the noblest survivals of early Norman work in the country. It has double aisles and the gallery at the triforium stage is carried round the north wall by an open bridge, presumably so that processions could pass round the church at this level. Its effect is that of a palace where from many levels guards, courtiers and servants watch the dramas of kingship – an impression that is not too fanciful if we remember the importance of Winchester, the scene of one of three annual crown wearings of the Norman kings, as a gathering for the court. The same pattern occurs in the south transept, but it is obscured by later accretions.

The Norman east end was completely remodelled in the thirteenth century by the building of the retrochoir and the Lady chapel (1205–c.1235). The presbytery arches were built in the first half of the next century, but all this work was much modified by the series of chantry chapels devoted to bishops of later periods and other changes. Of the Decorated period perhaps the most important remains are the stalls of 1308–10 by William Lyngwode. Gilbert Scott designed the present choir screen across the nave following the pattern set by Lyngwode, so that at first impression the stalls seem less ancient than they are. They are, in fact, the earliest complete set of wooden choir stalls to survive (there are earlier fragments at Rochester) with striking multifoiled canopies.

The great transformation in the old church came with the rebuilding of the Norman nave under two of Winchester's most celebrated bishops. The first of these, William of Wykeham (1367–1404), was Lord Chancellor of England and founder of Winchester College and New College, Oxford. The second was Henry Beaufort, Cardinal-Bishop of Winchester (1405–47), son of John of Gaunt and uncle to Henry V. The west front was rebuilt together with three bays of the nave in about 1360, but the main reconstruction began with William Wynford as the architect in 1394. It was completed with its vault in about 1450 by Robert Hulle. It was the last important work of its kind to be undertaken in an English cathedral. Begun rather later than Henry Yeveley's nave at Canterbury, it lacks the openness and frankness of Yeveley's masterpiece, and, like a complex and difficult piece of music, it needs and repays long study. For all its huge length, it gives the feeling of reserve, of some hidden secret of history – as though it were the chantry chapel of the Gothic spirit – a feeling conveyed both by the massive piers and the subtelties of the vault designs. Above the piers there still project the metal brackets from which tapestries were hung – a lost feature that must have added considerably to the grandeur of the nave and, because they were suspended,

Part of the Norman north transept

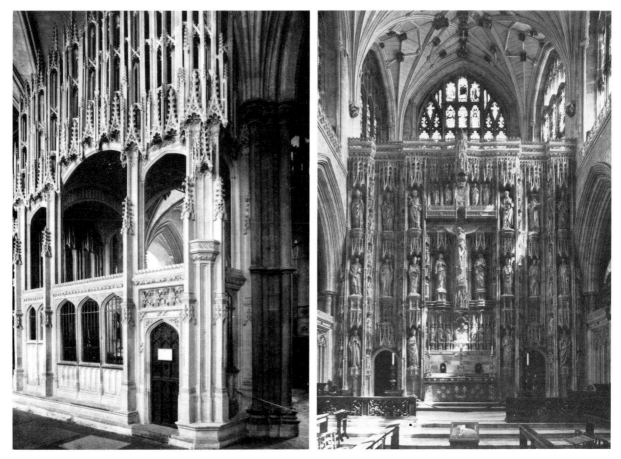

left: **Bishop Wayneflete's tomb** *and right* **The reredos of the high altar**

would also have alleviated the weightiness of the whole effect. (How this was achieved may still be seen, for example, in the tapestries hung in the nave of the cathedral at Como in northern Italy.)

Winchester is particularly rich in the chantry chapels of the later bishops, not only of William of Wykeham and Cardinal Beaufort, but also of Bishop Wayneflete and, most splendid of all, Bishop Fox, whose rotting corpse portrayed in stone lies in an embrasure of his chapel. It was Fox's architect, Thomas Berty, who completed the clerestory of the presbytery with its flying buttresses that now lights the magnificent late fifteenth-century reredos. Much good painting has survived at Winchester, notably the angels on the vault that give its name to the chapel of the guardian angels and the vault and wall paintings in the chapel of the Holy Sepulchre. What glass remains is largely a hodge-podge of fragments as in the west window. On the screens of the presbytery stand mortuary chests containing the bones of Saxon kings and bishops. When the Parliamentary soldiers ransacked the cathedral, they used the bones to hurl at the stained glass – grisly missiles for a grisly purpose.

Worcester

WORCESTER is the cathedral of Englishry. To see its tower rising against the Malvern Hills, where William Langland had his vision of *Piers Plowman* during the period of its construction, or to admire its prospect from the west as its image seems to dip deep into the river Severn, is to link oneself to that rich mood of place on which Sir Edward Elgar, another native of the region, so often drew in his music. To approach its exterior more closely is to suffer a disappointment, partly because nearly all the outer stonework is now Victorian and both the eastern end and the west front are replacements of the same period. Another, and less forgivable, disappointment is that since the war much of the medieval heart of the town has been torn down to make a noisy highway bordered by dull, characterless buildings.

Nevertheless, both the cathedral and the close, with its many monastic buildings, provide a rewarding complex to study. An atmosphere of learning

The south-west walk of the cloisters

far left: Inside the circular Norman chapter house; the windows were altered in the fifteenth century

left: Details of the lights, tracery and corner buttresses of the tower

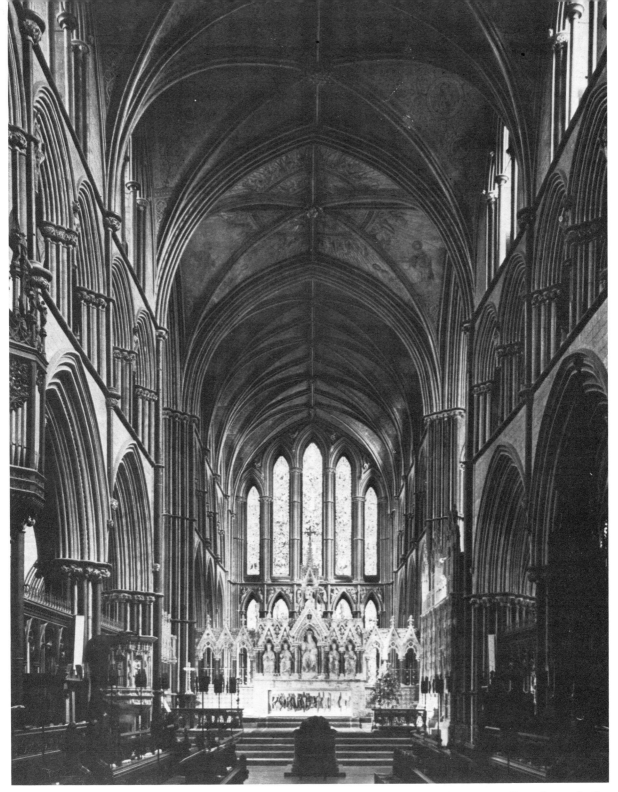

The choir, crossing of the eastern transepts, high altar, and Lady chapel: the lancets of the east wall are the work of A. E. Perkins in the last century, replacing a Decorated window

pervades the group of buildings which, with the intimate quadrangles of the close and the walled gardens, suggest an Oxford college with the cathedral as its exceptionally grandiose chapel. The tradition of learning goes back to St Wulstan, the Bishop of Worcester, who began building the cathedral in 1084, replacing the monastery church established by St Oswald who was made bishop in AD 961. Wulstan, who became bishop in 1062 – shortly before the Norman Conquest – was the only Anglo-Saxon bishop to retain his see under William the Conqueror. He believed that the Conquest was a rightful judgement on the English for their sins, a view he forcefully expressed in sermons still extant. By remaining in possession of his see, he was able to preserve much of the best of Anglo-Saxon ecclesiastical traditions in learning and in spirituality. He was, as much as the Norman-French bishops, caught up by the fervour for rebuilding of his time and, although he wept bitterly when it became necessary to pull down St Oswald's minster to build the nave of his new cathedral, he, nevertheless, allowed its destruction. Above ground little remains of Wulstan's cathedral – merely portions of the transepts – but the crypt which he constructed for the shrine of St Oswald is one of the most remarkable of all Worcester's architectural features. It is a wide, low underground chamber, its vaults supported by rows of slender, simple columns with plain capitals, marching up to a semicircular apse. A little later, in about 1120, the round chapter house with a central pillar that may have influenced the design of the later and Gothic polygonal chapter houses such as Lincoln was built.

The canonization of St Wulstan in 1203 greatly increased pilgrimages and

Sculptures in the south choir transept

gifts. King John, dying of a surfeit of peaches and cider at the other end of England in Newark in 1216, asked for his body to be buried at Worcester and here it still lies, encased in a tomb of carved Purbeck, with his effigy staring up at the vault. Beyond him rises the important work of the Lady chapel, begun in 1224 by Bishop Blois. As at Canterbury, great use was made of Purbeck marble so that the shafts give an impression of richness and variety. Purbeck is also used in the choir, whose rebuilding, begun by Blois, was completed by his successor, Bishop Cantilupe, the friend and supporter of Simon de Montfort. The Lady chapel and the choir are ascribed to Alexander Mason who, as John Harvey points out, may be the same Alexander who designed the nave and other important works at Lincoln. These two parts, which together with the eastern transepts make up the chancel, provide an interior of exceptional unity, an impression largely gained by the fact that the Lady chapel is the same height as the choir.

In the course of the fourteenth century the Norman nave was completely rebuilt except for the two western bays (these are Transitional work *c*1185), the northern side from 1320 onwards and the southern after 1350. The central tower by John Clyve was completed in 1374 and the present cloisters were erected in the same period. One great loss is that of the octagonal belltower erected outside the Lady chapel which rose with its spire to a height of over 200 feet. This was destroyed during the Commonwealth.

The cathedral from the river

York

YORK CAN EXPLAIN better than any other English cathedral city the relationship of the cathedral to the townsfolk. It preserves its extensive city walls, medieval streets, layouts and buildings, the halls of the guilds and numerous parish churches, many of which were built by and for particular trade guilds. Many of these trades would have come to the city for the first time because the construction of the minster attracted skilled craftsmen to settle there with the prospect of long employment. Once established there, they would continue to get work in the city and in the surrounding countryside. York thus reminds us of the importance of the cathedrals in promoting civic life and in attracting wealth to their cities.

York had, of course, a long and vital history before the coming of Christianity. As Eboracum, it was the capital of Roman Britain and the minster is built on part of the site of the legionary fortress. Here in AD 627 Paulinus converted Edwin of Northumbria and his court to Christianity. Edwin built a wooden oratory, later rebuilt in stone and added to by Wilfrid who was archbishop here. Under Alcuin in the eighth century the cathedral school gained international fame. Two Norman archbishops entirely rebuilt the minster on so much vaster a scale that it was probably the greatest church of its period in England after Old St Paul's. It was certainly bigger than Canterbury with whose archbishops the archbishops of York had such rivalry over the primacy of England. The excavations in recent years that accompanied work to strengthen the foundations of the central tower have revealed much about the construction of the Norman and earlier buildings on the site, and the curious visitor will find some of the results set out in exhibitions in the extensive crypts. The minster above ground today is, however, almost wholly Gothic and, as Sir Nikolaus Pevsner says '. . . for the Gothic style or rather styles in England, it tells us a more consistent and complete story than any other cathedral.'

There are two particularly exciting approaches to the minster. The first brings one to the glorious west front with the flowing tracery of the central window concentrated round the design of a heart and with its perpendicular west towers. The other is by way of the narrow streets leading from the Shambles to the south transept which suddenly rears up like a mountain face before us. The transepts are the earliest part of the Gothic minster; they were built between 1230 and 1255. They are very grand with double aisles but with one deficiency that applies to all the high vaulting of York; they are vaulted in wood, not stone. The dominating sight from the south entrance is the great lancet windows of the north transept, the Five Sisters, over fifty feet high and only five feet wide, with their thirteenth-century grisaille glass

Two of the sequence of the kings of England in the pulpitum

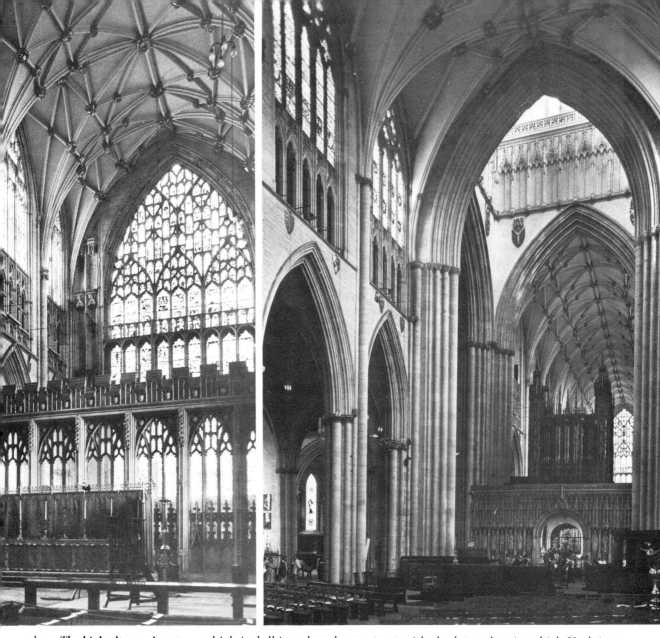

above: **The high altar and east window**

right: **The crossing and pulpitum from the nave**

which is dull in colour by contrast with the later glass in which York is so rich. The transepts are followed in date by the chapter house, the only polygonal one to be built, apart from Southwell, without a central pier. Here again the vaulting is of wood. It is a marvellous interior, fulfilling the boast of an inscription in Latin near the door, 'As the rose is the flower of flowers, so this is the hall of halls.' The ample windows are still rich with glass and the seats of the chapter overhung with canopies peopled with heads, a virtuoso performance in the depiction of the variety of human temperaments and moods. The vestibule, leading to the chapter house from the north transept, is in itself a remarkable construction, being one of the earliest attempts of that later Gothic ideal, to make a house of glass in which windows entirely supplant the walls.

The honey-coloured nave, built from 1291 onwards, also retains most of its glass. How it did so, when the fire of 1840 gutted the woodwork of the west towers and the high vault, was probably due to the protection given by the stone vaulting of the aisles. A dean of York in the last century reported that at a point when the fire inside illuminated with particular brilliance a crucifix in one of the windows, the soldiers, who were holding back the watching crowds, involuntarily presented arms. Infinitely improved by cleaning, the nave is impressive but not exciting. The feeling of excitement comes as we reach the crossing and see the series of English kings from William the Conqueror to Henry VI in the niches of the pulpitum. With shaggy hair and bolting eyes they stand upright as though startled out of their tombs by the last trump. They are all, except for the one of Henry VI (an addition of 1801), late fifteenth-century. Here our gaze shoots upwards into the lantern of the tower and the blaze of white light concentrated there.

Beyond the pulpitum stretch the choir stalls, good work of the last century, but replacing what must have been amongst the finest examples of their kind, lost in a fire in 1829 started by a maniac. The vaulting also was lost in the flames. Again, fortunately, the glass survived; particularly beautiful in the transepts of the choir, it amazes and delights by its extent and its wealth of colour. As we walk along these aisles, the transparency of the building works its magic upon us, so that our minds too are lightened as though the stone

below left: **The east front**

The exterior of the south transept

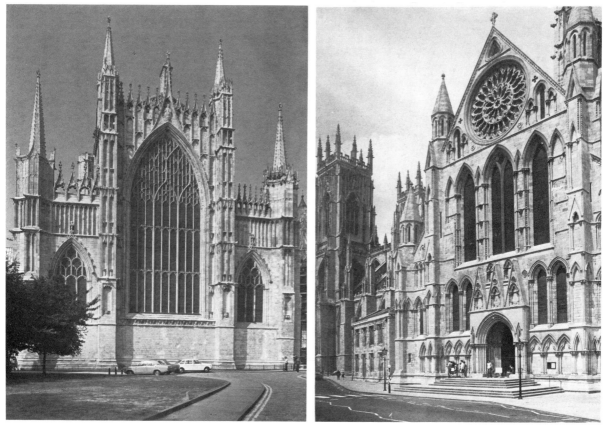

The wooden vault of the chapter house

walls of our habitual conceptions melted into traceries that let in the light of happiness. They also prepare us for one of the supreme pleasures of the minster – the great east window commissioned from John Thornton of Coventry in 1405 and telling the history of the world from creation to the Revelations of St John, all under the presidency of God holding a text proclaiming, 'I am Alpha and Omega.'

The Ascension: a wooden vault boss in the nave, Victorian work based on the original lost in the 1840 fire. Only Christ's feet may be seen and the marvelling apostles

far right: Looking up at a transept of the choir

Bangor

THE NAME BANGOR means 'wattle fence', the way in which St Deiniol, the first bishop here, marked off his sacred enclosure. This is the second oldest cathedral foundation in the British Isles, founded in about AD 525 and preceded only by that of St Ninian at Whithorn. Nothing survives of the early buildings and almost nothing of the Norman cathedral built by Bishop David, the Scot, in the early twelfth century. This was largely destroyed during the conquest of Wales by Edward I. Parts of the rebuilt cathedral, the transepts and the nave aisle walls, survive from the rebuilding begun in 1291 by Bishop Anian who baptized the first Prince of Wales (the future Edward II). This cathedral was also burned in the rising of Owen Glendower in 1404. In all weathers but the sunniest its exterior is dingy; the sandstone is black with grime and looks streaked with mould. The central tower is only a stump restored by Gilbert Scott and again in recent years, and the single west tower gives the building the impression of a parish church. After this, the interior, especially in the nave, is refreshing and spacious, with the steps from the west tower going down into the cathedral. This tower and the clerestory were added by Bishop Skeffington (bishop 1509–34) to the nave which had been remodelled a few years earlier. The choir and presbytery are full of heavy Victorian furnishings, although in the south transept are tombs said to be those of thirteenth-century Welsh princes. The most remarkable possession of the cathedral was acquired only in 1953; this is the early sixteenth-century wood carving known as the Mostyn Christ, here depicted as the Man of Sorrows wearing the crown of thorns and seated on a rock – a deeply moving work that may have come from one of the dissolved Welsh monasteries.

Below left: **Exterior of the nave showing** *(left)* **part of the west tower, and** *(right)* **the thirteenth-century crossing tower and transept: the tower showing above the parapet is that of the distant University College**

Interior of the nave looking eastwards

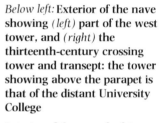

Llandaff

The Norman arch behind the high altar giving a view into the Lady chapel

THIS INTERESTING, SMALL CATHEDRAL was founded in 1107 by Bishop Urban on a site made holy in the sixth century by St Dubricius and St Teilo. Little of Urban's church remains. What is original in the choir, nave and west front is work dated 1193 to 1229. This was followed by the chapter house and the supremely elegant Lady chapel (1266–87). The aisle walls of the choir and nave are late fourteenth-century and in about 1500 the fine north-west tower, which owes much to the famous series of towers in Somerset under construction at the same time across the Bristol Channel, was built by Jasper Tudor, Earl of Pembroke, uncle to the reigning Tudor monarch, Henry VII. What we see now owes much to the Victorian restoration, largely carried out by the talented local architect, John Prichard, who added the spired south-west tower. By the early eighteenth century the cathedral had fallen into a dreadful state of decay: much of the nave was a ruin and in 1734 John Wood, the famous architect of Bath, was called in to build a Palladian church in the presbytery, known as the 'Italian Temple'. This, from the evidence of engravings, was a charming and skilful piece of work but it was pulled down during the restoration, to reveal among much surviving detail the Romanesque arch at the east end through which may be seen the only stone vaulting of the main body of the cathedral, that of the Lady chapel. Prichard also wholly restored the parapet and pinnacles of Jasper Tudor's tower. The nave is now dominated by a bridge bearing a statue of Christ by Sir Jacob Epstein. Built only a few years after the nave of St Davids, it is a completely Gothic design with none of the transitional features of that other cathedral. The square chapter house of 1244 is attached to the south side of the choir.

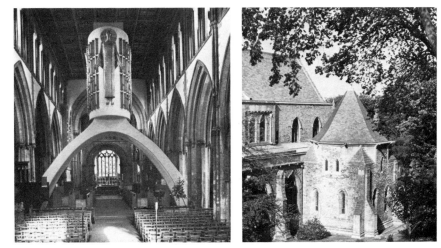

Epstein's Christ, mounted on a concrete bridge in the nave

far right: The exterior of the chapter house

St Asaph

THE AIR in this small town sited on a ridge between the valleys of the river Elwy and Clwyd is so pure that the tombstones outside the cathedral have their incised lettering illuminated by golden lichen. Here St Kentigern settled for a while in the sixth century before returning to Scotland where, confusingly, he is known as St Mungo (*see* Glasgow). He left behind him the first bishop, St Asaph, from whom the see and the town take their names. The Norman church was burnt in 1282 during Edward I's Welsh wars. The rebuilding was undertaken by Bishop Anian II who raised money by sending a famous manuscript of the Gospels on tour through the dioceses of Hereford, Lichfield and Wales to attract funds. The very plain nave, its piers rising without capitals to their arches, is of this period and so is the lower part of the tower. The choir is wholly a reconstruction by Gilbert Scott. Owen Glendower burnt the cathedral in 1402 shortly after the most impressive central tower was completed by the Chester mason, Robert Fagan. It is impressive for its very solidity and strength. For all its depredations and poverty, and almost because of them, St Asaph conveys a profound mood of endurance and spiritual resilience. It was fortunate in many of its bishops, the greatest of whom was William Morgan (bishop 1601–4) who, by translating the Bible into Welsh, helped to preserve an ancient civilization and a vital literature for a new age. He is buried in the cathedral and commemorated by a memorial in the graveyard outside.

below left: **View from the south-west showing the massively simple crossing tower**

Eastward view to the sanctuary from the nave

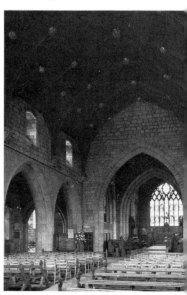

St Davids

ST DAVIDS, the shrine of the patron saint of Wales, is the only one of the four Welsh cathedrals to rival its English counterparts in scale and artistry. It is built beside a high bluff in the valley of the river Alan that runs to the sea and the host of islands off St Davids Head. Only the tower is visible from the small village and it is a splendid shock to pass through the gatehouse and to see the long body of the cathedral in its green setting spread out below. Here St David (cAD 530–601) became Bishop of Menevia (the old name of St Davids) after founding a monastery and travelling to Jerusalem. His foundation became an important centre for the training of missionaries to Ireland, and it was from the nearby Whitesands that St Patrick set sail for his work of conversion.

The cathedral now standing is said to be the fourth on the site since St David's time. As the Norman adventurers after the Conquest seized the southern coastline, intermarrying with the families of local princes and building a chain of castles that even now in Pembrokeshire marks the language barrier of English and Welsh, so the see of St Davids became a preserve of the new masters. It was under the third Norman bishop, Peter de Leia, that the nave and west front of the present cathedral were built between 1180 and 1198. A tower and choir were constructed at the same time, but in the thirteenth century that tower fell, severely damaging the choir and transepts. The builders obviously had great difficulty with the swampy site: the piers of the nave lean both outwards and sideways.

View up into the lantern of the tower

The west front was rebuilt by John Nash in the early nineteenth century. Inside, a most striking feature of the nave is its colour: it is built of a violet-coloured sandstone locally quarried that makes it both unique and very beautiful. Even though Wells was already under construction as the first completely Gothic cathedral in Europe, the transitional style of St Davids firmly continues the Romanesque tradition, not only in the round arches of the arcades and the clerestory windows, but in the thick ribbed, diamond-shaped and knotted mouldings of the arches. The only concession to the new style is in the pairs of pointed arches in the triforium, but even these are firmly held in obedience to the elder style by being recessed from the main wall so that each pair is grouped within the descending shafts of the clerestory windows. These arches have continuous mouldings like those in the nave triforium at Wells and it is possible that Somerset masons worked here. There are interesting carved roundels in the spandrels of the triforium arches. The coffered ceiling of the nave is much later (1472–1504) and is carved of Irish oak. From the corners of each coffer hang crenellated pendants like castles floating in the air, each joined to one another by a fretted arch. It is a construction of astonishing richness that fully complements the stonework below it.

A view across the nave, showing the round arches of the arcade and the clerestory and the pointed arches of the triforium

Passing beyond the early fourteenth-century pulpitum that masks from the nave the choir stalls of about 1470, we come to the presbytery and east crossing, begun in 1221, and the later work made necessary by the fall of the Norman tower. The spatial relation of choir to high altar is particularly fine. Before the high altar stands the enamelled brass slab of the tomb of Edmund Tudor, grandfather of Henry VIII, who had it moved here when he dissolved the friary at Carmarthen in which it originally stood. To the left is the shrine of St David, and high on the screens flanking the altar steps are, like those at Winchester, elegantly fretted Jacobean mortuary chests containing the bones of ancient Welsh princes. Here, indeed, is a place where great strands of history meet and where violence, ambition and the vicissitudes of life are reconciled by the redemptive power of art.

The choir aisles lead to the retrochoir and the Lady chapel (begun 1296) which suffered greatly after the Reformation and was heavily restored by Gilbert Scott. An interesting feature of the east end of the cathedral was that the retrochoir went round an open courtyard at the back of the presbytery. Presumably it was left open to provide the lancets behind the high altar with light. This space was filled by Bishop Vaughan who used it between 1509 and 1522 to construct the small perpendicular chapel of the Holy Trinity, with its exquisite fan tracery perfectly scaled to the proportions of the whole. There, in a recess cut into the east wall of the presbytery, is a casket containing the bones of two men said to be St David and St Justinian. These were found during Gilbert Scott's restoration in the last century and, as St David was said to have been of great stature and one of the skeletons was of a big man, it is

General view of the cathedral from the south-east. The ruins of the Bishop's Palace are on the left

left: **Piers and arches of the choir from the south aisle** *and right* **The shrine of St David in the north choir aisle**

fair to conjecture that here, still preserved, are the mortal remains of the patron saint of Wales whose shrine makes two pilgrimages to St Davids worth one pilgrimage to Rome!

The great feature of the exterior is the tower whose middle stage is mid fourteenth-century and which was raised to its present height of 125 feet also under Bishop Vaughan between 1509 and 1522. It is singularly plain for its period and its designers disdained the use of corner buttresses, thus endowing it with a majestic simplicity. They allowed themselves only the luxury of pinnacles and a pierced parapet. To the south-west of the cathedral stand the ruins of the Bishop's Palace, the construction of Bishop Gower in about 1340, the most splendid building of its type to survive anywhere in the British Isles. The same purple stone that was earlier used for the nave was here employed in a chequerwork pattern (with white stone) along much of the upper reaches of its exterior. Here too survives in large part the great hall, the chapel and other apartments around the courtyard where hundreds of pilgrims once gathered and where their modern descendants also find a welcome for the spirit.

opposite above: **The spired and fortified towers of the west front**

opposite below: **Granite drum piers in the nave with, above, some of the shields of the heraldic ceiling**

Aberdeen

THE CATHEDRAL OF ST MACHAR at Old Aberdeen has lost its crossing, transepts and choir and now consists only of a nave and west front; for all that, it is a remarkable and fascinating building. A cathedral was built here in about 1157; nothing remains of it. What is now the east wall contains the fourteenth-century columns of the crossing; the rest is fifteenth- and early sixteenth-century. It has two striking features: the west front and the roof of the nave. The west front consists of two fortified towers with slit fenestration and machicolation linked together by a west window with seven tall lights and a portal beneath. Bishop Gavin Dunbar (1518–32) replaced the original cape-house roofs of the towers with squat sandstone spires, obviously attempting to alleviate their grim, defensive aspect but also to make them fit with the spire of the now vanished central tower. Impressive and intriguing rather than beautiful, this front sums up the tensions in Scottish society in the later Middle Ages, the yearning for civilization expressed not only here but in the University of Aberdeen founded by Bishop Elphinstone in 1495 and the lawlessness of a territorial nobility seated in their castles.

Gavin Dunbar, who built the spires, was also bishop when the wooden ceiling of the nave was made. The nave itself with seven bays and round granite piers harks back to Romanesque forms, but the ceiling is utterly of its period. It contains forty-eight heraldic shields set out in a way that conveys the patriotic Scots view of Europe in about 1520. The centre line of shields begins in the east with the arms of the Medici Pope Leo X and continues with those of the contemporary archbishops and bishops of Scotland, ending with the arms of Aberdeen University. Prominent among those of the bishops is the red heart of Douglas, placed there for the poet-bishop of Dunkeld, Gavin Douglas. The north line of shields portrays all the monarchs of Europe, beginning with the black eagle of the Holy Roman Emperor, then Charles V, whose other arms as king of Leon and Castile, Aragon, Navarre and Sicily are also shown. Henry VIII's arms are displayed shorn of the lilies of France, a deliberate rebuttal of England's claims to the French throne. The southern row begins with James V of Scotland and continues with the arms of various royal kinsmen and noblemen ending in those of the Royal Burgh of Aberdeen. In this ceiling, probably planned by a canon of the cathedral, Alexander Galloway, and executed by the craftsman, James Winter, the whole of Europe on the eve of the Reformation is depicted through the compressed language of heraldry. The independence of Scotland is proclaimed by the fact that the king of Scots and his noblemen are given the side of honour, the south side of the cathedral which was the side of the Holy Ghost. James V is proclaimed emperor within his realm and free of English domination. What a history lesson, what a work of art!

Brechin

THE MOST NOTABLE FEATURE of Brechin is its round tower, one of only two surviving on the Scottish mainland – the other is at Abernethy. The Brechin tower has been dated on documentary evidence to AD 990–1012. Its appearance here denotes the infiltration of Irish Christian influence into the country of the Picts. The tower which is 87 feet high has a carved doorway surmounted by a crucifix in the Irish manner with the legs of Christ uncrossed. On either side of the door are ecclesiastics, one holding a T-headed pastoral staff, Coptic in origin, and the other a Celtic crook. The cathedral into which this important monument was incorporated was founded by David I in 1150. Like most Scottish cathedrals, it suffered particularly badly in the Reformation and later. The thirteenth-century choir was ruined but substantial portions including some fine lancet windows remained to be repaired and reroofed in 1902. The transepts were demolished in 1807. The nave which has thirteenth-century piers was fortunately retained as the parish church. The west front with its thirteenth-century portal and a later west window survived, as did the strongly built projecting tower built between 1351 and 1373. The spire of this tower is later in date.

below left: **The round tower and south side of the cathedral**

Early carvings of a crucifix *(above)* **and of ecclesiastics on the sides of the raised entrance to the round tower**

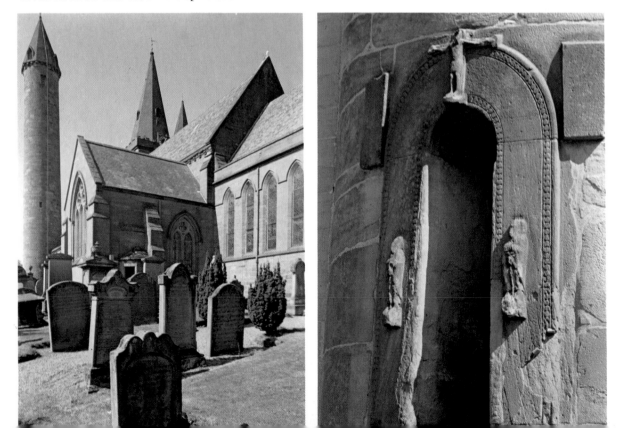

Dunblane

THIS PERTHSHIRE CATHEDRAL set beside the river Allan was a particular favourite of John Ruskin. It takes its name from St Blane who built a church here in the sixth century. Made a bishopric by David I in about 1150, Dunblane has a square tower of this period added to in its upper stages in the thirteenth and fifteenth centuries. Under the Dominican Bishop Clement (c 1233–58) who raised the necessary funds with papal sanction, the present cathedral was begun and largely built. The thirteenth-century buildings here include the choir, the Lady chapel, the west front and, perhaps, much of the nave. The nave roof fell in during the sixteenth century and it was not until 1893 that it was restored. The west door is particularly fine, with acutely pointed blind arches on either side, and with twelve orders of shafts and mouldings whose richness has been increased rather than diminished by the pittings and striations of wind and rain. Above the west window is the leaf-fringed *vesica*, or pointed oval opening, which Ruskin particularly admired. The broad nave with its eight bays has no triforium but a fine clerestory with an inner and outer wall making a passageway at this stage. Among the cathedral's furnishings, which include the tomb of an Earl and Countess of Strathearn, is an unusual survival for a Scottish cathedral – six of the richly carved stalls made for Bishop Chisholm (1486–1534) with luxuriant foliation about their ogival canopies and with misericords.

left: **The west front with Ruskin's window in the gable**

below: **The richly moulded thirteenth-century west door**

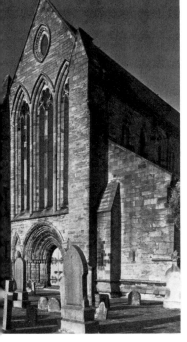

Dunkeld

SET IN A BEAUTIFUL wooded Highland valley beside the waters of the river Tay, Dunkeld was founded as a see by Alexander I in 1107 on a site first made holy by the visits of St Columba and St Mungo. The present cathedral consists of a choir much rebuilt in the last century but containing thirteenth-century work and used as the parish church and of an important fifteenth-century ruined nave. The aisleless choir contains some interesting features including a lepers' squint, the window by which these unfortunates could watch the celebration of the mass. To its north is a chapter house long used as the burial place of the dukes of Atholl. It is the ruined nave and its north-west square tower that command attention. Considering its condition, this nave, begun under Bishop Cardeny in 1406 and consecrated by Bishop Lauder in 1464, retains much of its detail. The plain round columns are reminiscent of the nave of Aberdeen, but here there is a triforium of round arches topped by a clerestory of pointed windows with *flamboyant* tracery. Similar windows flank the aisles. The west window built over a gallery above the door is odd in that it is off-centre – presumably because at some stage it was enlarged. The cathedral contains two notable altar tombs, one that of Bishop Cardeny and the other said to be the resting place of the villainous Wolf of Badenoch who destroyed Elgin Cathedral. The greatest figure associated with Dunkeld is one of its last bishops, Gavin Douglas, the translator of Virgil and a poet and writer of astonishing evocative gifts.

below left: **The ruined nave and the north-west tower**

below centre: **A view across the nave showing the rounded triforium arcade**

The west door

Edinburgh

For all the many changes to its structure – its exterior, apart from the crown on the tower, was completely remodelled in the 1820s and earlier had been divided into four churches – St Giles seems alive with history. It is one of the great stages in the architectural progression of the Royal Mile that leads down from Edinburgh Castle to Holyrood House – and the crown of its tower, made by eight pinnacled ribs joining to support an intricately carved spirelet, is one of the most memorable and enjoyable of late Gothic achievements. The closed crown which it imitates was reserved for emperors alone: its use here (in 1495) is an assertion of the independence of Scotland, a theme which inspired the nave ceiling at Aberdeen Cathedral. Of the interior nearly the whole of the existing building is fifteenth- or sixteenth-century. Only the piers of the crossing may include work from the Norman church of St Giles of about 1120 which was destroyed by Richard II of England in 1385. The crossing makes little interruption to the flow of nave and choir into one another. They are spacious and wide, having in many aspects the effect of double aisles from the addition of wide chapels such as the Preston aisle. What contributes greatly to the grandeur of the interior is the height of the piers, many of which have capitals finely carved with shields and heraldic devices. The Preston aisle is named after Sir William Preston who gave the church the precious relic of one of St Giles's arms in 1454. Another addition was the Chepman aisle, given by the man who in 1507 introduced printing to Scotland; he and his wife were buried in it.

The pre-Reformation appearance of the church with its forty-four altars must have been particularly sumptuous – and the celebration of St Giles's Day, 1 September, was one of the great events of the city. Then with the Reformation everything changed. The statue of St Giles was thrown into the loch below

The famous spire of St Giles which, imitating the closed crown of an emperor, asserts the independence of the Scottish kings

The west front

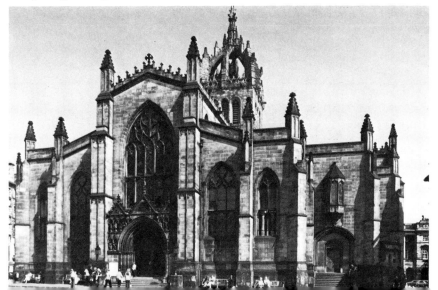

The choir seen from the
Preston aisle

the castle known as the Nor' Loch; John Knox was made minister in 1559 and
the church saw many dramatic scenes in the struggles between the
supporters of the old religion and the new. Charles I, in his ill-fated attempt to
restore episcopacy to Scotland, made St Giles into a cathedral in 1633. In
1637 Jenny Geddes hurled her stool at the dean, so annoyed was she at
hearing the English service being read, one of the incidents that led the next
year to the signing of the National Covenant. Under Charles II and James II St
Giles was again a cathedral, but then reverted to the Presbyterians after the
Glorious Revolution. It was after this that it was divided into four. Between
1872 and 1883 it was restored to its present form. The chapel of the Thistle, a
romping exercise in Gothic pastiche, was added in 1911. All the glass is now
nineteenth-century or modern. St Giles, however, is rich in monuments,
notably those of the Marquess of Montrose, hanged, drawn and quartered for
his support of the Royalist cause in 1650, and his great enemy the Marquess
of Argyll, beheaded after the Restoration in 1661.

Elgin

ELGIN WAS ONCE one of the grandest cathedrals of Scotland and it is now one of her grandest ruins. The bishop of Moray moved his see here in 1224 and portions of the earliest building remain in the façade of the south transept. A bad fire in 1270 did much damage to the as yet incomplete building which then underwent much modification. Worse was to follow when Alexander, brother of Robert III, known as the Wolf of Badenoch, quarrelled with Bishop Baw and descended with his highlandmen in 1390 to pillage, burn and destroy whatever they could in the cathedral. In the bishop's letter of complaint to the king he spoke of his cathedral as 'the special ornament of the realm, the glory of the kingdom, the delight of foreigners and stranger guests.' Once more the cathedral was restored, reaching its final form only in 1538 when a great central tower was erected to replace a fallen predecessor. That tower too fell in 1711 crushing the nave and north transept, but for long the

below right: **The chancel interior: two tiers of lancet windows, five in each, surmounted by a rose window**

The twin towers and the empty frame of the west window above the main portal

The central pier and vaulting of the chapter house

cathedral had already stood roofless. The lead had been stripped from the roofs in 1568 and the rood screen was broken up in 1640 on the orders of the General Assembly.

Among the chief remains are the west front with its twin towers and a great doorway and window between them, the south aisle wall of the nave and the south transept, the choir and the east end and a detached chapter house. The cathedral was not particularly long – about 260 feet – but it had one feature in its nave that reveals a strong French influence; it had double aisles, fully developed at Chichester alone of the other cathedrals considered in this book. These were probably first planned after the fire of 1270 and further carried out after 1390 because they do not fit into the earlier scheme of the towers of the west front. Far more survives here than at St Andrews, the other great artistic loss among cathedrals caused by the Reformation in Scotland. There is, for example, the thirteenth-century octagonal chapter house, the only one of its kind in Scotland, finely vaulted and provided with a central pier after the ransack of the cathedral in 1390. The two great architectural triumphs of Elgin are the west front and the chancel with its east end. In the centre of the west front is the richly moulded portal with, above it, the west window, robbed of its tracery and open like a mouth protesting at the desecration. On either side stand the bare west towers with their tremendous buttresses, making bold shadows to the height of the surviving stages. The whole combines to make a grim and unforgettable image. Equally memorable, but with a more piercing quality in its ruinous state, is the eastern wall of the chancel with its two tiers of exquisitely framed lancets, five in each tier surmounted by a rose window in the gable which is flanked by canopied turrets topped by octagonal pyramids. It is one of the most superb compositions of the late thirteenth century, simple and assured in plan, and subtle in composition and detail.

Door with bold dogtooth ornament into the south transept

Fortrose

THIS NORTHERN CATHEDRAL on the promontory of the Black Isle was the see of the bishops of Ross, who removed here from Rosemarkie in the early thirteenth century. If little remains of it, that is because Cromwell's men used it as a quarry to build their fort at Inverness. Apart from the undercroft of the detached thirteenth-century chapter house, what still stands is the south aisle that extended alongside both the vanished nave and the choir. The division between the aisles of nave and choir is marked by an octagonal belfry tower. Although the main body of the church was thirteenth-century, this aisle is later, the gift of Euphemia, Countess of Ross, whose tomb is traditionally said to be that in the easternmost arcade. The second of her husbands was the Wolf of Badenoch, and on his death in 1394 she took the veil and became abbess of the convent of Elcho. One of the vaulting bosses displays the arms of Bishop Bullough who held the see from 1420 to 1429. The scale of the vaulting, when so many Scottish cathedrals and great churches in more populated regions had to be content mostly with wooden roofing, is an indication of the wealth that was lavished on its construction.

below right: **Exterior of the remains showing the octagonal turret**

Vaulting and tomb embrasures in the remaining south aisle of the cathedral

Glasgow

THE FIRST CATHEDRAL was founded by St Mungo, that indefatigable gentleman we have already met under his other name of St Kentigern at St Asaph. On a journey from Culross he came upon a dying Christian called Fergus. Having comforted him, he put the dead man's corpse on a cart which was drawn by untamed oxen. The oxen were allowed to wander at will and they halted at a cemetery earlier established by St Ninian. Here Fergus was buried where the aisle known either as the aisle of Car Fergus or as Blacader's aisle now stands, and Mungo started his settlement. Two Romanesque buildings were followed by the Gothic cathedral which is largely the work of Bishop de Bondington (1233–58) under whom the crypt, the choir and the tower were built. The arrangement of the crypt and choir is unique; the crypt held the tomb of St Mungo while above in the choir of the upper church his relics were preserved in a shrine behind the high altar. The nave was begun in the early fourteenth century but was not completed for many years. Under Bishop Lauder (1425–47) the stone spire was set on the tower and the thirteenth-century chapter houses were remodelled and completed. In 1472 Glasgow was raised to an archbishopric. Archbishop Blacader (1483–1508)

View up the nave towards the pulpitum and the lancets of the east end

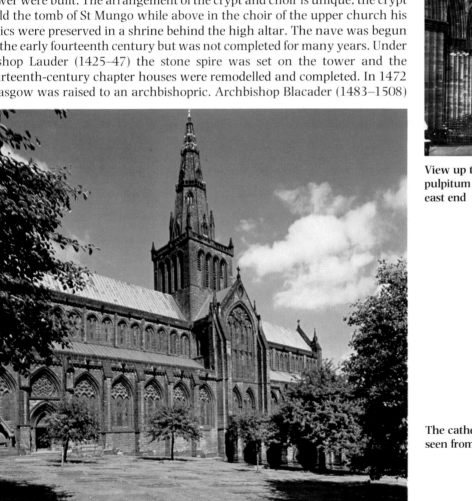

The cathedral with its spire seen from the south-west

Piers and vaulting looking towards the site of St Mungo's tomb in the crypt or lower church

The nave from the crossing showing the disposition of the triforium and clerestory

built the stairs from the crossing to the crypt, the pulpitum and the aisle which bears his name.

The nave is simple and well-proportioned but it is at the crossing that the originality of Glasgow is first displayed. Stairs flow down and rise up in many directions, down in wide flights on either side to the crypt, up to the short transepts and to the door in the pulpitum leading into the choir. Everything invites, intrigues, affords speculation. The stepped effect is confirmed by the two massive stone altar bases on either side of the stairs up to the choir entrance. The pulpitum with its traceried parapet, obviously influenced by the French *flamboyant* style but undeniably of the late Gothic Scots national style is particularly fine and a worthy preparation for the thirteenth-century choir. The choir is a noble interior with its richly moulded arches, the foliage on many of its capitals and the acutely pointed arches in the bays of the east end. Through these arches can be seen the ambulatory of the retrochoir with subsidiary chapels built out over the crypt. The crypt is even more remarkable. Its focus is the tomb of St Mungo surrounded by four pillars supporting the stone vault like a massive canopy; these again are grouped about by rows of alternating thick and thin piers. West of the tomb was a space for pilgrims; east was the Lady chapel which now opens into the far east end with four chapels. It is one of the most complex and rewarding of all Gothic interiors.

Iona

THE FIRST SIGHT of this cathedral on its tiny island across the Sound of Iona from the Ross of Mull is unforgettable. After the vast volcanic landscape of Mull and the harsh red granite of the Ross, Iona shines with brilliant white beaches and low green hills, a place of peace where beauty and holiness are one. Even across a mile of water the cathedral, with its 70-foot tower and its pitched roofs, clean-cut in the Hebridean light, seems enormous in comparison with the small houses of the straggling village, whose Gaelic name means 'the great city'. Here one feels the joy of journey's end as a medieval pilgrim must have felt it and here too one realizes, as in few other places in Britain, the contrast of size that the abbeys and cathedrals of the Middle Ages presented as against the ordinary secular architecture of the time.

The prestige and the hallowed atmosphere of Iona derive from St Columba, the Irish saint, who came there in AD 563 and founded a monastic settlement from which the northern Picts of Scotland were converted to Christianity and which later sent St Aidan and other missionaries to the conversion of Northumbria and the founding of Lindisfarne. It is, therefore, a place of fundamental importance in the history of the civilization of Britain and even

below left: **View of the cathedral looking towards the Sound of Mull**

Looking across the choir to the sacristy

Pier and half-arch of the choir south aisle

above right: **Crosses before the much restored west front**

now is considered to be the chief repository of Celtic Christian art, notably in its crosses and tombstones, many of which are now kept in the fourteenth-century church of St Ronan on the way to the cathedral. So holy was the island that forty-eight kings of Scotland, Ireland and Norway were buried there. Macbeth is one of these kings.

In the twelfth century communities of Benedictine monks and nuns were established on Iona and the present cathedral, which is largely of the late fifteenth and early sixteenth centuries, incorporates elements of the twelfth-century abbey. A cruciform building, whose details and furnishings suffered badly from the centuries when it stood roofless (after the Reformation to 1905 when its restoration was completed), it was made a cathedral in 1506 when the Bishop of Argyll moved here from Lismore (*page* 176) and established the bishopric of the Isles. The nave is aisleless, but attached to its north-west corner is an ancient oratory which according to tradition held the shrine of St Columba. The piers of the south choir aisle and those half-embedded in the north wall that separates the sacristy from the choir all show that archaizing tendency of late Scottish medieval building which we have already noted at Aberdeen and Dunkeld. The capitals, though weatherworn, retain some interesting carvings. The cathedral and the restored cloister and other monastic buildings are now the centre of the Iona Community. Much is owed to the Community for the present impressive atmosphere of the interior. What conveys, however, the strongest effect is the exterior of the cathedral with the varied and remarkable tracery of the windows of the tower and the great crosses standing on the green before the west front – the sense of a living tradition that makes the visitor confirm Dr Johnson's words written after he came here on his famous Highland jaunt with Boswell. 'That man is little to be envied, whose patriotism would not gain force upon the plain of Marathon, or whose piety would not grow warmer among the ruins of Iona.'

The west front

Kirkwall

EARL MAGNUS was murdered on the island of Egilsay in 1117 by his cousin, Hakon, with whom he shared the earldom of the Orkneys. For want of another executioner Hakon had ordered his cook to kill Magnus who told the cook to strike him on the forehead so he might die like a chieftain and not be beheaded like a thief, saying to him, 'Take good heart, poor wretch, for I have prayed to God for thee, that He be merciful unto thee.' Magnus's body was buried in the small cathedral whose remains still stand on the tidal island of the Brough of Birsay. The manner of his death, memories of his life and a series of miracles performed at his tomb convinced many that he was a saint, including the Bishop of Birsay, William the Old. By the manner of his life Magnus had introduced a new spirit into the heroic barbarism of the Norsemen of Orkney. In 1129 Magnus's nephew, Rognvald, made a bid for the earldom and his father, Kol, advised him to make a vow promising to build a great church in Kirkwall to be dedicated to St Magnus if he were successful. He won the earldom and kept his vow; the work, supervised by Kol and carried out by masons of the school of Durham, began on the new cathedral in Kirkwall in 1137.

Door in the north aisle of the nave

The see was transferred from Birsay. There are few better examples of the change of scale brought about in ecclesiastical architecture in this period than the comparison the remains of the tiny cathedral on Birsay, built about 1050 for Earl Thorfinn, make with the cathedral of Kirkwall. Not large by English standards, its dark red sandstone form soars over the small, pleasant town. Originally the choir terminated in an apse, but this was removed when the choir was later extended. The parts that would appear to have been built in Rognvald's lifetime were this choir, the first crossing and the transepts. On Rognvald's death in 1158 he was buried in the cathedral where now the shrine of St Magnus stood. Rognvald, poet, lover, crusader and magnanimous ruler, was also canonized – first by popular regard and then with papal sanction – one of the few instances of a man being made a saint because he was such a splendid fellow. At the Reformation his bones and those of St Magnus were hidden in piers of the choir – to be rediscovered in later years. Under Bishop Bjarni, another poet and author of the *Lay of the Jomsvikings*, much of the nave was built. By the end of the twelfth century the crossing was rebuilt and between 1220 and 1230 the work on the first stage of the west front with its three doors and that on the extension of the choir took place. Later building included the central tower with a spire of the fourteenth century (the present spire was built in this century) and the completion of the west front.

This west front with its red stone flecked with yellow sandstone is one of the rare examples in these islands of the deliberate striving for polychromatic effect through the patterning of different coloured stones. Its early Gothic portals lead respectively into the aisles and nave of the cathedral. This front suggests extreme breadth for what lies within and it is a great thrill to pass inside and receive the shock of the vertical emphasis of the nave, so high in proportion to the narrowness of the centre aisle. The colour of the stone calls to mind images of blood, but of blood as the river of life, not as the signature of death; there is a vivid Northern energy about this interior that is intensely moving. Remarkably for a great church so distant from the main sources of skilled workers, all the high vaulting, except in the transepts, is of stone – simple Gothic vaults that with the pointed arches of the crossing marry naturally with the Romanesque drum pillars and rounded arches of the bays and the triforium. This interior combines the spirits of the patron of the cathedral and of its founder: Magnus's courage to forgive and Rognvald's adventurous life-accepting zest. Durham masons certainly worked here in the twelfth century and probably Frenchmen in the next; they responded, however, to the natures of their Norse patrons and their work provides one of the finest examples of how a cathedral, through being the shrine of great heroes, could preserve and refine the aspirations of the people it served.

It must be remembered that for nearly the whole period in which significant additions were made to Kirkwall, it, with the rest of Orkney, was a dependency of the kings of Norway. St Germanus on the Isle of Man was the only other Norse cathedral in these islands. Earlier the bishops of Orkney had come under the archbishop of Hamburg; in 1152 they were made answerable to the Norwegian archbishop of Nidaros. It was only after Orkney fell to the Scottish crown in 1472 that the see was placed under the archbishop of St Andrews. After the Reformation in Scotland bishops came and went with the vicissitudes of the Stuarts in the distant south until the episcopacy was abolished in 1690. After much neglect the cathedral was restored in the last century and in this. It is now well cared for, but one can only regret the loss of the tombs of the Norse earls and notables, as well as the shrines of the two saints, not just for their historical and pious associations, but for the vigorous Scandinavian sureness of line and boldness of invention with which they must have been decorated.

The west doors of the cathedral

St Andrews

FORMERLY THE GREATEST CATHEDRAL in Scotland, St Andrews is now vaulted by the sky and spired by the clouds. The only remains are the west door and one tower of the west front, part of the south aisle wall and the south transept and the east wall, together with ruins of the monastery of the Augustinian regular canons whose priory was attached to the cathedral. The rest of the masonry is now incorporated into the houses of this delightful town which extends westwards from the promontory on which the cathedral stands overlooking the North Sea. How the early Christians here first came to possess relics of the apostle, Andrew, is a question more obscured than illuminated by myth. According to one story a Syrian monk, St Regulus, was instructed by an angel to filch parts of St Andrew's anatomy when the Empress Helena was not looking and to set off for the island of Thule. He arrived at this promontory and founded a settlement. Another legend gives the eighth century for the arrival of the relics. However they came, these relics were to be of the greatest importance in the emergence of Scotland as a nation. In these relics of an apostle the Scots had something the hated English did not have, and the symbol of St Andrew's martyrdom, the saltire or the

left: **The east wall framed in the doorway of the west front** *and right:* **The portal of the chapter house, seen from the cloister**

cross set on its side on which St Andrew was crucified, became the national flag of Scotland. By the early thirteenth century St Andrews was declared free of obedience to York whose archbishops had claimed the right to consecrate the bishops and, although not raised to an archbishopric until 1472, it had for centuries been considered the primatial see of Scotland. In the War of Independence St Andrews and the surrounding country was one of the chief centres of resistance. In 1318 King Robert Bruce was present with all the bishops and nobility of Scotland at a service of consecration. In 1418 Bishop Wardlaw founded the university, the oldest in Scotland – an example to be followed in the same century by prelates at Glasgow and Aberdeen.

The tower of St Rule (or St Regulus)

The cathedral remains stand within a wall nearly a mile in perimeter that also enclosed the priory buildings and the remarkable church of St Regulus with its tall, square tower built by Yorkshire masons in about 1120. The cathedral was begun in 1160 and in its finished state by the early fourteenth century was 355 feet long with a central tower and spire. The fragmented west and east fronts answer to each other across a sad void with stumps of stonework marking where once the piers rose. The twelfth-century east front retains its lantern turrets and an east window with stubs of tracery inserted in the fifteenth century, making a proud and magnificent screen. Almost more moving are the remains of the west front, built between 1273 and 1279, with its wind-eaten door and one fine south turret supported by a flying buttress and corbelled out from the west wall. North and east of this turret broken-off arches yearn to continue into windows or the arcade of the lost triforium and imagination is forced to recreate and extend what these fragments can only hint at – a building of the highest quality. Various remains of conventual buildings are left within the precinct, including the portal arches to the chapter house.

How could a creation so wonderful, so essential to the pride and historic tradition of Scotland have been allowed to sink into such decrepitude? Unlike similar cases in Ireland, the English cannot be blamed. The Scots did it themselves – largely because of the hatred of episcopacy that was aroused by the savage Beatons, archbishops of St Andrews, the first of whom was James Beaton, archbishop both of Glasgow and St Andrews, regent of Scotland in the minority of James V. The second was his nephew, the cardinal-archbishop David Beaton. They both persecuted the early reformers mercilessly. Three of the most notable of these, Patrick Hamilton, George Wishart and Walter Myln, were put on trial inside the cathedral and then were burned outside the archiepiscopal castle. Shortly after Wishart's burning in 1546 Cardinal Beaton was murdered within the castle and before his mistress's eyes by friends of the martyr. The tide turned in favour of reform. In June 1559 John Knox preached four sermons on the 'Cleansing of the Temple', advocating the destruction of images and tearing the veil of belief from the minds of his hearers. The building itself was not attacked; it was merely allowed to decay, and in less than a hundred years it was a largely roofless ruin.

Annaghdown

ON A NARROW ROAD beside Lough Corrib in County Galway all that Annaghdown seems to present from the outside is the plain roofless ruin of its fifteenth-century cathedral. On entering the ruin, you come upon the glorious surprise of a late Romanesque window brought, perhaps, from an earlier church and inserted in the chancel. Whether it was transferred from an earlier cathedral on this site or from the priory whose ruins exist a little distance apart is a matter of conjecture. This priory was granted to Augustinian nuns in 1195 who took over a monastery originally founded by St Brendan for his sister in the sixth century. Carved in a fine blue-grey limestone, the window is exceptional both for its width and for its unity of design; richly ornamented chevrons bite into the moulding which is the immensely long body of a monster. Its hindlegs are at the base of the right-hand jamb and its head on the other side devours a bundle of serpents. What it signifies is mysterious; it is there and very beautiful. As with so many of the Irish cathedrals which are now ruins and where only a few features survive, instead of overwhelming the visitor by a mass of detail, Annaghdown affords in this window one marvellous and memorable experience. The very isolation too of these places aids the aesthetic explorer in his concentration as it once helped the saints and monks in their devotional exercises. Annaghdown was taken over by the archbishopric of Tuam in 1321 but kept its bishops to the end of the fifteenth century.

below right: **The exterior of the ruined cathedral**

The Romanesque chancel arch with its design of the long body of a monster

Ardfert

A SITE OF GREAT RICHNESS, Ardfert includes a cathedral, two churches and not far off a Franciscan friary. Situated in a part of Kerry that was colonized by the Anglo-Normans, the cathedral is largely thirteenth-century; it was probably built between 1252 and 1256 under Bishop Christian who was a Dominican, and it may owe its form to his earlier experience as a friar because it much resembles a friary church. His building incorporates in its west front part of an earlier church on the site. This consists of a doorway flanked by blank arcades, all in a much decayed soft sandstone. Enough survives, however, to reveal the influence here of Cormac's chapel at Cashel. The arch of the inner order of the door rises from triple columns to chevrons in the voussoirs. In the outer order the chevrons point outwards. The round tower which stood before this west front no longer exists.

The particular beauty of what remains at Ardfert lies in the chancel with its tall, thin lancets in the east wall and the nine lancets making an arcade of the south wall. Apparently the nave was, by contrast, very poorly lit, so that the impression would have been of advancing from darkness into a brilliantly lighted chancel. Ardfert demonstrates what could be achieved by Gothic architects in Ireland, working with infinitely poorer financial resources than in England and in, of course, far less settled conditions. They could not build to a comparable height, they were rarely able to vault their churches or to use the

The Romanesque west door and blind arcade

left: Interior showing eastern lancets of the chancel and the arcade of windows in the south wall

right: Temple na Hoe, a Romanesque church associated with the cathedral

View of the thirteenth-century chancel from the south-east. Note the defensive stepped crenellations in the parapet

three stage elevation, and they could not vary their wall surfaces with intricate clusters of columns and tracery. Therefore, they preserved the vertical élan of the Gothic in the basic simplicities of the style in, for example here, the bold way in which the three lancets of the east end are taken right out into the gable. Similarly the widely splayed nine windows of the south wall with their trefoiled rear arches give an impression of variety that goes far beyond their comparatively simple construction. The emphasis on the vertical and the adoption of wide splays for inner embrasures were both notable features of the Irish Transitional style, especially in the west, as we shall see at Kilfenora where the tall lights are given round arches. The Ardfert east windows are a natural extension of this style, once the pointed arch was fully accepted. In the niches bordering the lancets of the east end are carvings of later bishops, one of whom is said to be of Bishop Stack who died in 1488. Later work includes the addition of stepped battlements, almost certainly for defensive use in about 1400, the sacristy building and the south wing.

North-west of the cathedral the church known as Temple na Hoe contains some later Romanesque carving and the unusual feature of columns at each corner of the nave. The chancel has disappeared. Beyond Temple na Hoe is the fifteenth-century church of Temple na Griffin, so called because of the griffins carved inside it. At about the same time as the cathedral was rebuilt, a Franciscan friary was founded nearby, probably in 1253. The church here was strongly influenced by the design of the cathedral, even to the provision of nine lancet windows in the south wall of the chancel. Further additions were made in the fourteenth and fifteenth centuries, and after the Reformation the church was used for a time by the Protestant bishop of Ardfert.

Ardmore

ARDMORE IN COUNTY WATERFORD can boast in its founding saint of St Declan, who was, as bishop in Munster, already bringing the gospel to the Irish before St Patrick arrived. An early oratory, known as St Declan's house and traditionally the site of his burial, stands to the east of the ruined cathedral. The cathedral was built by Moelettrim O Duibh-rathra who became bishop here and died in 1203. He probably incorporated part of an older church in his building which consists of a nave with a chancel later extended eastwards. The windows and arcading of the interior are of the Transitional period, although the pointed chancel arch may be later. The most remarkable feature lies in the sculptures on the outside of the west wall. They are set in arcades, the lower ones within wide arches depicting among their subjects Adam and Eve, the Judgement of Solomon and the Adoration of the Magi. Among those in the upper band, which are much harder to make out, is the Archangel Michael weighing souls. These sculptures are of the same date as the cathedral. Although much worn, they have an appealing naiveté and on occasion, as with the kneeling figures (*below right*), considerable grace. It is extraordinary to reflect, however, that they are contemporary with work like the chancel arch at Annaghdown which, drawing on the native Irish tradition of interlaced ornament and fantastic animal depiction, is infinitely more sophisticated.

The other great feature of the site is the round tower of Ardmore, retaining its conical top and reaching a height of 95 feet. Probably twelfth-century, it is one

below left and centre: **Details of the carvings on the west wall of the cathedral showing Adam and Eve and a man kneeling before a standing figure**

The round tower with the ruins of the cathedral on the left

Carvings in the blind arcade of the west wall of the cathedral

of the last, and best preserved, of the series of round towers that were first constructed in the ninth century in response to the Viking raids and which remain in large numbers as notable features of many of the cathedral and monastic sites. Their purpose and their age were both the subject of fierce debates in the last century. It is now agreed that they performed several functions: they were belfries from which the monks in the fields were called in to services; they were stronghouses for keeping monastic treasures; and they were places of refuge to which the abbot and monks could flee when attacked whether by Vikings, rival monasteries or Irish kings. This is why the entrance is nearly always many feet above ground level; once the monks got in by ladder, they could draw it up after them and wait in hope that their attackers would go away. The last time the Ardmore tower was besieged was in 1642 when the English caught elements of the Catholic Confederate Army here and, on their surrender, hanged over a hundred of them on the spot.

Detail of the carving above showing the three Magi

Cashel

Cormac's chapel, showing the two towers and the exterior of the chancel

THE CATHEDRAL OF ST PATRICK together with its surrounding buildings and monuments – the early cross of St Patrick, the round tower, Cormac's Romanesque chapel and the great perimeter wall – crowns the massive limestone slab of the Rock of Cashel that rises out of the plain of Tipperary with a magnetizing presence, quickening the heart of the traveller as he catches his first glimpse. Here, in the mid fifth century, St Patrick baptized Aengus, the young king of Munster, on the spot where the cross now stands. It is said that during the baptism the saint drove the sharp pointed staff on which he was leaning into Aengus's foot. Afterwards he noticed the wound he had inadvertently made and asked why Aengus had not complained. Aengus said he thought it was part of the ritual.

Cashel remained in royal hands, although it was frequently fought over – Brian Boru, the great high king of Ireland who led his countrymen against the Vikings to be killed at the moment of victory at Clontarf in 1014, was crowned king of Munster here in AD 977. It remained in his family, and in 1101 an O'Brien king made a grant of the Rock to the Church 'for God, St Patrick and St Ailbe' and Cashel became a centre of the Reform movement in Ireland. With the twelfth-century reorganization of the Irish Church Cashel became one of the four archbishoprics of Ireland. The great artistic achievement of this period of prosperity was the marvellous chapel built by Cormac MacCarthy between 1127 and 1134. This was a work of seminal importance for Irish architecture; the architect would seem to have known not only English and Norman work, but also Rhineland churches such as the abbey church at Murbach in Alsace on the west bank of the Rhine. This Benedictine monastery had many Irish connexions. Brian de Breffny in his recent discussion of the chapel suggests that the architect was a well-travelled Irish Benedictine who came into contact with Cormac at the school of Lismore where Cormac stayed in 1126. Tiny by

Cormac's chapel: the interior showing the chancel from the nave

The cathedral showing (*left to right*) **the fortified west end of the nave, the south door, the central tower, and the south transept**

English and continental standards, it epitomizes a number of up-to-date Romanesque features such as the twin towers, the ribbed vaulting in the chancel, the blind arcading, at the same time combining them with certain native Irish elements such as the stone roofs. These stone roofs are sharply pitched, that of the chancel stepped down in two stages. The nave roof contains an upper chamber like that at St Flannan's oratory at Killaloe (*page* 169) which probably

The north transept and part of the round tower, and (*left*) the crossing looking towards the chancel

Heraldic beasts

St Peter: a detail of a tomb carving

Beasts and foliage on a tomb

derives from this one. The external walls are richly decorated with blind arcading and a series of human heads peep out from the eaves. The two square towers which give the chapel a cruciform ground plan are particularly reminiscent of Rhenish work. Originally the main entrance was by the north door, a magnificent archway, now overshadowed by the later cathedral. Inside there is more blind arcading and carving, particularly in the chancel arch. The nave is tunnel vaulted and the chancel has ribbed vaulting. A splendid stone sarcophagus of unknown provenance, but showing strong Norse influence in its carving, is a worthy addition to this harmonious and intriguing church.

A new cathedral was built later in the twelfth century, but this was entirely replaced in the thirteenth century by the present building beside which Cormac's chapel now nestles. It is clear that the architects and their patrons wished to preserve as much as possible of the venerable past as they oriented the new cathedral in such a way that Cormac's chapel was contained in the angle of the south transept and the choir, while the round tower was attached to the north-east corner of the north transept.

This cathedral was built under three archbishops, Marianus O'Brien, David MacKeilly and David MacCarvill, between 1224 and 1289. Its wooden roofs have long gone and much of the fabric has fallen or been demolished. The choir is much longer than the nave which, perhaps, was never built to its full length. Its most beautiful feature is the crossing, the finest in Ireland, which retains its vaulting and the fourteenth-century tower overhead. Many good late medieval tombs survive, particularly in the transepts. The north and south walls of the choir were both provided with arcades of splayed windows, rather like those at Ardfert. As the builders progressed westwards from the crossing, they used limestone rather than sandstone for capitals and other carved portions and there is much interesting work, foliage and human heads among them. More impressive than any individual feature is its atmosphere, one of overwhelming sorrow. Other Irish ruins are softened by the landscape about them; here because of the elevated site there is nothing to see from inside the cathedral but the sky, which remorselessly emphasizes its ruined state. Green mould crusts the stonework, revealing where the rain most habitually weeps and the faces bordering lancet windows mourn for what might have been.

The reasons for its ruined state can be traced first to the extraordinary construction at the west end, which is a castle built in the fifteenth century to protect the archbishops in a particularly unruly period. Even that did not save them because in 1494 the Earl of Kildare burned the cathedral. Summoned to Henry VII's presence in London to explain his outrageous deed, he excused himself by saying that he only did it because he thought the archbishop was inside, an answer that so pleased Henry that he made him viceroy of Ireland. The internal quarrels of Ireland were soon to be intensified by the Reformation. The archbishop appointed by Elizabeth I, Myler McGrath, trimmed between the old and the new religions, dying a Catholic at the age of a hundred. His tomb is to be found in the chancel. Further depredations were caused in the wars of the seventeenth century, but the building's final doom was settled by an eighteenth-century archbishop who, annoyed that his carriage and horses found difficulty in getting him up the sloping road to the Rock, had the roof removed. A new, elegant Palladian cathedral was built in the town below, conveniently situated near the archiepiscopal palace.

Clonfert

IN THE CARVINGS of its west door the tiny cathedral of Clonfert in County Galway possesses the masterwork of the Irish Romanesque. If a pilgrimage to one of the grander shrines described in these pages still allows one to acquire merit in the afterlife, then the very difficulty of the twisting journey to Clonfert – on which time and again the visitor is sure to lose his way – brings a reward equal to few in this world. Decaying woods of an ancient demesne frame two sides of the graveyard and a ruined lodge stands by the gate to make with the cathedral and the deserted countryside around as sequestered a place as the most romantic soul could ever hope to find.

It is right, however, that it should be hard to get to because this is the foundation of that famous traveller, St Brendan the Navigator, who started a monastery here in AD 563. The earliest parts of the cathedral, including the west door and the ruined south transept, are twelfth-century. In the fifteenth century a belfry tower, reminiscent of the towers erected by Franciscan convents of this period, was placed above the west front. In the same century a new chancel arch was added. It has charming carvings of angels, of a mermaid with her looking glass and comb and delicate rosettes and leaf sculptures. This arch now acts as a frame to the earlier twin lights of the east windows of the chancel. These, very like the chancel windows of O'Heyne's church at Kilmacduagh, have blind arcading in their wide splays and are framed within rolls of superb craftsmanship. Dated to the second quarter of the thirteenth century, they are in their abstract purity a fitting contrast to the complexity of the west door which was probably made in about 1170. Built of warm red sandstone, it consists of eight orders of jambs all inclining inwards, surmounted first by seven orders of arches and then by a triangular pediment bordered by carving like rolled ropes or cables. Above the apex of the pediment two human heads protrude from the wall. In the pediment itself ten more human heads, some bearded, some young and shaven, appear between triangles with richly carved ornamentation. Below this stage more heads are contained in the arches of a blind arcade immediately above the outermost order of the arch. The orders of the arches exhibit an astonishing variety of ornament, among them interlacing, enormous bobbles, deeply cut formalized flowers, beast heads and elegant rounded and engraved cusps. The capitals are a zoo of animal heads, cats, horses, donkeys and dragons, and the jamb shafts or pilasters on which they stand are an anthology of mingled Celtic and Romanesque decoration. The innermost order of the door is a fifteenth-century replacement, not in sandstone, but in blue-grey limestone. A strange contrast not only in that it also contains naive carvings of an abbot and a bishop and a scroll of vineleaves with an angel clutching the tendrils at the apex, a theme that for all the primitive style of the carving immediately

South-west view of the cathedral showing the west door and above it the fifteenth-century belfry

right: **The west door**

Mermaid with comb and looking-glass: a carving in the chancel arch

evokes the strange man amongst the vineleaves at Southwell (*page* 99). This later insertion does no damage to the whole impression of the portal, which seems of staggering complexity as one stands back from it and tries to take in its form set in the lichenous and mortar-rendered wall. With its triangular pediment, it looks like the frontal elevation of a gabled and roofed projecting porch – the north porch at Wells, for example. Either the funds were lacking to build such a porch or the nameless genius who made it was interested only in the sculptural possibilities of such an elevation. Doorways such as this reflect Christ's words 'I am the door' and, thus, meant the entry into the life of Christ. This portal is a scheme of Christ in creation with the Trinitarian theme of the pediment repeated in the triangles separating the human faces of the redeemed that project above the animal heads, the vegetable forms, the zoomorphic interlacings and the contortions of the mineral world in the arches, capitals and shafts below them. It is a diagram of the redemption of matter – a theme worthy only of a supreme artist with the power to bring the complexity of his imaginings to order. Here at Clonfert theme and artist met.

Clonmacnois

THE CATHEDRAL HERE is one of a flock of grey churches that seem to graze on a green mound beside a broad reach of the river Shannon on the County Offaly bank. The site projects towards the river from a range of peaked hillocks. It is a place of singular beauty with its eight ruined churches, its two round towers and its great stone crosses, the remains of one of the most famous monasteries and one of the greatest centres of learning of Celtic Christianity. It was founded by St Ciaran who died in AD 548 at the age of thirty-three. He was the friend of St Columba of Iona and St Kevin of Glendalough and all the records of his life and the many legends that accumulated round his name reveal the charm of his nature. Animals loved and obeyed him; a pet fox would carry in its mouth to and from his tutor the wax tablets on which his school lessons were written and the hide of his cow which followed him when he left home was long preserved here as a precious relic. He came to Clonmacnois because of a dream he had when studying on one of the Isles of Aran. He dreamed that a great tree grew in the middle of Ireland with fruit-bearing branches sheltering the central plain. Flocks of birds flew to it to eat its fruit and to carry the fruit to distant lands. His friend, St Enda, interpreted the dream by telling him that he was the tree, that all Ireland would be filled with his name and that foreigners would be fed by his prayers and fasting. He

Dean Odo's door

The tenth-century Cross of the Scriptures, standing before the west front of the cathedral. On the right is one of the many churches on the site

was to go forth and found his church by the banks of the Shannon, in the centre of Ireland as the dream indicated. To give one example of the fulfilment of this prophecy, the Anglo-Saxon Alcuin of York, the leader of the Carolingian Renaissance, came here to study in the eighth century and, obviously at his bidding, the Emperor Charlemagne sent great gifts to Clonmacnois. Neither the Vikings nor the Irish were quite so kind; it was plundered six times between AD 834 and 1012 and burnt twenty-six times between AD 841 and 1204. During one Viking occupation the leader of the expedition placed his wife on the high altar where she prophesied and carried out pagan rites. Time and again the monastery recovered until, in 1552, the English garrison at Athlone bore all the valuables away and, apart from a short revival in the seventeenth century, the site fell into its present state of ruin.

The first cathedral was built here by Abbot Colman in the early tenth century. This was replaced by the present structure which is probably the work of Cormac, son of Conn, and Flaherty O'Lynch in the late eleventh century. It is a single-chamber church with antae at both ends: the earliest feature is the fragmentary west door. In 1189 the last high king of Ireland, Roderick O'Conor, was buried in the sacristy that preceded the present seventeenth-century sacristy. In about 1460 Odo, the dean of the time, had the north door inserted. It is a work of exceptional beauty, particularly for the fineness of its mouldings and the figures of St Dominic, St Patrick and St Francis above the arch. At about the same time the chancel was divided into three altar bays and vaulted, but unhappily this is now ruined. Outside the west front stands the famous tenth-century Cross of the Scriptures and

The South Cross and O'Rourke's tower

below right: **The Romanesque west door of the Nun's church**

The round tower and chancel arch of Temple Fhinginn with a view of the river Shannon beyond

One of the many Celtic tomb slabs now preserved in an open-air gallery at Clonmacnois

beyond that the round tower known as O'Rourke's, begun in about AD 960 and completed in the twelfth century. To the north-west of the cathedral is the tiny oratory in which St Ciaran was said to have been buried. Here two croziers, one of which is said to have been St Ciaran's own, were excavated. There are three other churches built close to the cathedral. At the bottom of the slope towards the river is the Romanesque church and round tower known as Temple Finghin. Eastward of the cemetery wall which encloses the cathedral and these churches is the Nun's church with fine Romanesque carvings to the door and chancel arch. Westwards is the ruin of a thirteenth-century castle.

Cloyne

THE MOST MEMORABLE FACT about Cloyne is that the philosopher George Berkeley was bishop here from 1732 to 1753. He was very fond of Cloyne for the peace and seclusion he found there – and so quiet and deserted is it still that many a philosopher today would find it beneficial to retire to. Dedicated to St Colman MacLenon who died about AD 600, the present cathedral, a cruciform building, dates from around 1270. It has been very much altered. The chancel arch was blocked up in the early eighteenth century and then removed altogether in 1775. The curious roofs of the nave and aisles which slope down almost continuously were arranged like this in the early eighteenth century when the battlements were removed. There are good lancet windows in the transepts; in the north transept there is an ugly marble memorial to Bishop Berkeley. The graveyard contains the remains of an oratory said also to have been a fire house like that at Kildare. Over the road from the cathedral stands a round tower which has lost its cap.

The interior of the nave   **Exterior of the south transept and the chancel**

Dublin

DUBLIN HAS TWO MEDIEVAL CATHEDRALS – Christchurch and St Patrick's. The first cathedral on the site of Christchurch was founded while Dublin was still a Norse town by the king of Dublin, Sitric Silkbeard, whose bishop was called Donat. When the Anglo-Normans seized Dublin in 1171, their leader, Strongbow, joined the archbishop of Dublin, St Laurence O'Toole, in a scheme to rebuild the cathedral. Archbishop O'Toole had already – in 1162 – converted the organization of the cathedral from a secular chapter to a foundation of Augustinian regular canons. On his death in 1180, his successor, the Anglo-Norman John Comyn, built a palace outside the city walls and beside it the collegiate church which was to become the cathedral of St Patrick in 1192. It is likely that Comyn and his successors found it

below left: CHRISTCHURCH: **view down the nave to G. E. Street's chevet**

CHRISTCHURCH: **the north side of the nave, showing the most original disposition of the triforium and clerestory**

difficult to get on with the Augustinians at Christchurch who, nevertheless, fought hard to retain their privileges and dignities. Following the disestablishment of the Irish Church in the last century, Christchurch was made the sole diocesan cathedral of the Church of Ireland for Dublin, while St Patrick's is regarded as the national cathedral of the Church of Ireland. The possession of two cathedrals has probably impoverished Dublin rather than otherwise – because, frankly, neither cathedral is in the front rank and it would have been far better if the resources available (which were obviously quite considerable) had been devoted to one building of exceptional splendour.

Apart from the transepts, the entire exterior of Christchurch is restored or is, from the crossing, the work of George Edmund Street, the architect of the Law Courts in London who created a French chevet-like eastern termination attempting to replace the original form. The south side of the nave collapsed when the vault fell in 1561 and this he rebuilt to the style of the north side. The transepts and the crypt are what remain of the church of St Laurence O'Toole who, dying in exile at Rouen, asked for his heart to be sent back to his cathedral. This is said to be in an iron heart-shaped case preserved in the chapel of St Laud. The best remaining parts of the cathedral are the extensive crypts, which, containing so many fragments of the medieval church, are like a charnel house of Irish Gothic, and the north side of the nave. This latter

CHRISTCHURCH: **exterior showing the tower and south transept**

CHRISTCHURCH: **in the crypt**

part, built between 1212 and 1235, is particularly rich in carving, reminiscent, as is only to be expected from the Somerset masons who built it, of Wells. They brought their stone from the quarries at Dundry near Bristol from which they shipped it to Dublin. What is wholly original here is the arrangement of the triforium which is united with the clerestory stage in a brilliant and unique solution. Marble shafts rise from each opening of the triforium straight up to the clerestory level and the trefoil headed arch of the centre opening in the triforium is repeated in the clerestory.

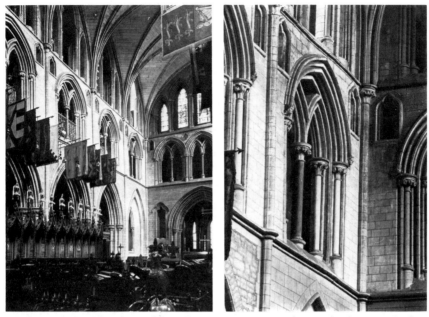

far left: ST PATRICK'S: **the banners of the Knights of St Patrick hanging in the choir**

left: ST PATRICK'S: **a detail of the choir triforium**

ST PATRICK'S: **eastward view from the nave**

The interior of St Patrick's is far more austere. This is the largest Gothic church in Ireland – 300 feet in length, and H. R. Leask, the historian of Irish ecclesiastical architecture, suggests that the patrons and architects aimed at size at the expense of ornament and interesting decoration. The exterior shows the restorer's hand throughout, except in the massive north-west tower named after Archbishop Minot who built it in the fourteenth century. It is capped by a spire and provided with restored stepped battlements. The restoration within and without was paid for largely by that munificent brewer, Sir Benjamin Lee Guinness, from 1864 onwards. George Bernard Shaw thought his architect was the devil in person. Nevertheless, Frank O'Connor who devotes some marvellous pages to the cathedral in his *Leinster, Munster and Connaught* finds it a deeply moving building and suggests that no one should pass judgement on it until he has attended a service there. What is immediately attractive about the interior is the important series of eighteenth-century monuments: the view up the north aisle of the nave, for example, with its standing marble figures and, most thrilling of all, the bust of Jonathan Swift and the epitaph he wrote for himself – the greatest in history said Yeats – saying that he has gone 'where savage indignation may no longer lacerate his heart'. Yet another aspect of St Patrick's that helps to make it the repository of national history lies in the sight of the crests and swords of

ST PATRICK'S: **Minot's tower, the west front, and part of the nave exterior**

the now defunct Order of St Patrick which adorn the stalls in the choir with the bright banners hanging overhead. Of the original building constructed between 1220 and 1224 the most authentic remaining portions are the three eastern bays of the north side of the nave, the vaulting of the south transept with its eastern wall and aisle and the north and east walls of the choir. The much restored Lady chapel is said to have been influenced by Salisbury, at whose consecration in 1224 the archbishop of Dublin of the time was present.

Ferns

FERNS IN COUNTY WEXFORD has a charming name, an ancient and important history and the remains of a monastery and a castle, as well as parts of the thirteenth-century cathedral now incorporated in the Church of Ireland church of 1817. It was a seat of the kings of Leinster, one of whom, Dermot MacMurrough, founded an Augustinian monastery here in 1160 where he later died, rotting alive, as his enemies said, because it was he who invited the Anglo-Normans to Ireland to solve his own political difficulties and, thus, began the long and fateful domination of Ireland by her neighbouring island. Ferns became a centre of the Anglo-Norman settlement. The castle was built in about 1200 and the cathedral was begun probably by the first Anglo-Norman bishop, John St John. It was probably intended that this cathedral should be on the same scale as Kilkenny. Burnt in 1577, by the time of its rebuilding in 1817 only the presbytery, parts of the transept and the belfry remained. Some original lancet and vesica windows of the presbytery remain. Eastward there stand parts of the south and north walls of what seems to be the choir of another church with arcades of lancets. What purpose this church served, whether it was the choir of the Augustinian abbey or the chapel of the shrine of the first founder of the monastery, St Aidan, is not clear.

The cathedral with *(right)* **the ruined choir of another church**

Glendalough

THIS IS ONE OF THE WONDERS of Ireland: a secluded place in the granite mountains of Wicklow, with two lakes set among wooded slopes and with what appears to be a cascade of ancient churches flowing down the valley. Desiring complete eremitical solitude, St Kevin came here in the sixth century and found a cell for himself in a cave that may only be reached by boat on the upper lake. The earliest churches on the site were constructed beside this lake, but with the progression of time the community, as it grew and flourished, moved down the valley. The ruined cathedral is one of a group of ecclesiastical buildings, including a round tower built within a perimeter wall or 'cashel' which retains its gate, the only surviving gateway to an Irish monastic enclosure. What survives of the cathedral is its nave, chancel and sacristy. The cathedral was built probably first in the tenth century and its nave is 30 feet wide, the widest of any early church in Ireland. The remains of this early work are the lower courses of large stone blocks in the nave, the antae and the lintelled west doorway. The upper parts of the nave walls are later; the chancel – which may well have replaced an earlier chancel – is twelfth-century and so, probably, is the sacristy. Grouped close to the cathedral are other buildings of considerable interest, including St Mary's church (tenth- or eleventh-century), the rounded tower, a small building

below right: **The cathedral showing the chancel arch and chancel from the nave**

The round tower

St Kevin's Church

A stone cross

called the Priest's house and the well-known St Kevin's church with its short round tower which is eleventh- or twelfth-century. Furthest down the valley is St Saviour's priory said to have been founded by St Laurence O'Toole in 1162. He was made abbot here in 1153 and later, as archbishop of Dublin where he rebuilt Christchurch, he incorporated the diocese of Glendalough in his archdiocese.

Perhaps because of being enclosed in the mountains, Glendalough preserves more than any other monastic site of comparable importance the sense of what it was like to be a member of one of these learned and holy communities in the Dark Ages. In the now vanished cells that surrounded these churches, students were taught, manuscripts were copied and, if they were to be books of ritual significance, such as the *Book of Kells*, which were carried in procession and displayed in church services, ornamented with the wonderful enlacements of Celtic art with a skill that has never been recaptured. Among the monks too were goldsmiths and silversmiths capable of the finest work, executing the same designs in filigrees and chasings of the precious metals of their trade. Surviving examples, such as the Ardagh chalice and the silver mounted croziers and reliquaries, confirm contemporary accounts of how crammed these small churches were with riches and decoration. They were frequently plundered by raiders and every time the monks had to make good the loss and damage. Such was the vitality of the community here that Glendalough lasted nearly five hundred years, fulfilling its role as one of the seedbeds of Western Christian civilization.

Kildare

THE FORTIFIED AND CRUCIFORM cathedral of Kildare is too severe a building to stand on the site of the monastery founded here in AD 470 by St Brigid. So holy was this lady that the very sunbeams acted as hooks from which to hang her wet cloak to dry, and when at Kildare she was granted as much land as her handkerchief would cover, it miraculously expanded to spread over the land she needed for her monastery. Cogitosus' biography of the saint of about AD 630 describes the great church in his day: probably of wood, it was decorated with linen hangings and paintings on the panels; the east wall had two entrances, one for the bishop and one for the abbess and her nuns. The monastery here grew to be one of Ireland's great centres for learning, numbered with Clonmacnois, Ferns and Glendalough in the prologue of the ninth-century Calendar of Aengus the Culdee, and many of the most influential Irish emigré scholars to the continent came from here. In the twelfth century the infamous Dermot MacMurrough attacked the monastery and forced the abbess to marry one of his followers – one of the events in his life (another being his own abduction of Devorgilla, the wife of Tiarnan O'Rourke) that led to his immense unpopularity and his calling in the Anglo-Normans.

After the invasion Kildare became the seat of the powerful Fitzgerald family

The cathedral from the north-west showing the defensive character of the building, with arches for machicolation and stepped parapets

The round tower and the western bay of the nave

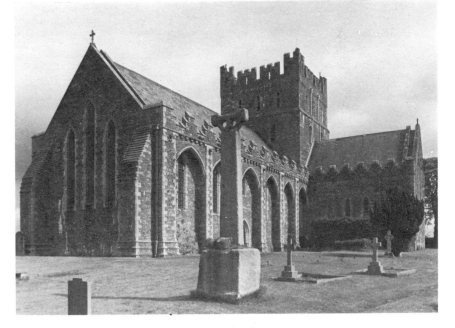

and the cathedral was built to its present form from 1223 onwards by Bishop Ralph of Bristol. Of what is to be seen now the chancel, the north transept and the west wall are the work of George Edmund Street in the last century. The impressive central tower was also heavily restored. All the windows are lancets. What is both important and interesting is that it is a fortified church. The nave is provided with the earliest form of stone machicolation, consisting of arches joining the buttresses with a space between the wallwalk and the parapet for dropping missiles. The provision of steps up and down the roofs next to the gables meant that the defenders could rush rapidly to whatever section of the building was threatened. The parapets carry the stepped battlements, characteristic of later medieval Irish ecclesiastical architecture, which are said to be an introduction from Spain. These are about 1395 in date, though again much restored. There are some fine Fitzgerald tombs, particularly in the south transept, and some floortiles.

West of the cathedral is a round tower with a Romanesque doorway; its cone was replaced with battlements in the eighteenth century. North of the nave are the foundations of what is called St Brigid's fire house. Here a sacred fire was kept perpetually burning by the nuns after her death. They would tend it by rota for nineteen nights and leave it to the saint herself to mind on the twentieth night – it never went out – and then the cycle would begin again. As well as its ritual significance, such a fire house would provide a practical need in times when fire could be fetched from it for the rest of the monastery.

The crossing and chancel seen from the nave

Scenes of the Passion on a tomb

Kilfenora

Tomb slab of a bishop in the chancel

SET IN A HOLLOW OF THE HILLS close to the Burren Mountains, the cathedral of Kilfenora is dedicated to St Fachtna who founded a monastery here. There was an early stone church here and four crosses, the most important being the Doorty cross with its carvings of bishops, a bird devouring skulls and Christ on a donkey entering Jerusalem. Another cross was removed from here to Killaloe in 1821. Kilfenora was created a bishopric in 1189 and the cathedral appears to date from about 1200. It is small and simple, consisting of a nave walled off to form the Church of Ireland cathedral and a chancel which is ruined, as are other parts to the north. The east wall of the chancel contains three tall lights with the round tops typical of this period of Irish Transitional architecture in the west. The piers, carrying narrow shafts between moulding, have carved capitals, one with formal foliage and the other a curious group of clerics praying with intense fervour. Two tomb slabs are set up in the chancel, one of a bishop, and the other of what the guidebooks call a prelate – probably for want of any other name to give to this extraordinary freak who looks like the creation of a science-fiction writer. What no guidebook mentions or describes is the magnificent head of a bishop projecting above the south door of the nave; comparable to some of the best work in England of the thirteenth century, this head, by suddenly reminding one of great Gothic figure sculpture, is all the more startling for its appearance in this forlorn spot.

The ruined chancel showing the tall transitional windows

Kilkenny

St Canice's at Kilkenny is the cathedral church of the see of Ossory, the oldest Irish diocese, having been founded at Saige in Offaly in AD 435. The see was moved here when St Cainneach or Canice established his cell on one of the two hills that dominate this fascinating Anglo-Norman town with its many medieval remains beside the river Nore. On the other hill is the castle built by William Marshal who married Strongbow's daughter and heiress. The castle came into the hands of the Butler family, Lords of Ormonde who rose to a dukedom and declined to a marquisate, many of whose tombs stand in the cathedral.

This is one of the best Irish cathedrals from several points of view, position, preservation and richness of intrinsic detail and furnishings. A round tower stands beside the south transept. An earlier cathedral was burned in 1085 and in 1114. Then, following the firm establishment of Anglo-Norman domination over the surrounding region, the English bishop, Hugh de Mapilton (1251–56), began the present cathedral which was probably largely

left: **The north aisle looking westward with a view of the nave**
The thirteenth-century west door

The south side of the cathedral

above right: **The effigy of a lady of the Butler family**

St Peter with his keys: a tomb carving

completed by 1280 under his successor Bishop St Leger. It is a cruciform church with a south porch, transepts and chapels, that act as aisles to the chancel, running off the transepts. It also possesses a fine west door. The east end of the chancel extending beyond these chapels is extremely well lit by three pairs of lancets. The Lady chapel, now the chapter house, is even better lit; this was completely rebuilt in the restoration of 1866 using the old materials. At the same time the chancel which had been separated from the main body of the church was brought back into use. The hideous pointing of its masonry would appear to be the work of later restorers. That is the only severe blemish of restoration in this remarkable building. Because it was largely built in one period of construction it conveys a powerful sense of unity, increased not only by the agreement of style but also, because there is no screen, by the uninterrupted view from nave to east windows. At the base of the interior west windows is a curious arcade above the west door which may have been used as a gallery in Easter services. The nave is constructed in five bays with piers of quatrefoil plan 20 feet apart making spacious divisions. The clerestory windows are unusual in their quatrefoil shape. The crossing was much rebuilt after the original tower fell in 1332 and was rebuilt. Its lierne vaulting with holes for bell ropes is fifteenth-century. Through the choir we reach the great lancets of the east wall, once filled with glass thought so remarkable that in 1641 Rinnucci, the papal legate come to advise the Catholic Confederation who had risen against the English, offered to buy them. His offer was refused and a few years later they were smashed by Cromwell's soldiers. For some reason they left largely untouched the remarkable series of sixteenth- and seventeenth-century Irish late Gothic tombs, notably those of the Butler and Mountgarret families, with armed knights and ladies in horned head-dresses and robes of stone made to flow as though channelled by water. The sides of these altar tombs, one of which is ascribed to a noted member of a family of tomb sculptors, Rory O'Tunnell, contain fine carvings, as well, of saints, crucifixions and emblems of the Passion.

Killaloe

ST FLANNAN'S CATHEDRAL stands beside the river Shannon at the point at which it issues from Lough Derg on its way to Limerick and the sea. The view offered from the other side of the water is particularly beautiful, whether the tower and the eastern wall and windows of the chancel is reflected in the river or whether the water is flowing fast and the extreme verticality of the east windows contrasts with the rapid stream below like an emblem of eternity above the current of time. An earlier cathedral on this site founded by St Molua, who was followed here by St Flannan, was almost totally destroyed. A Romanesque doorway of exceptional quality from this earlier building was incorporated into the extreme south-west corner of the nave, which was completed in about 1225. Why this doorway was turned inside out, so that the voussoirs intended for the exterior of the old church now face the interior is a minor mystery. Next to it stand a Viking stone carved with the same message in both the ancient Irish and Scandinavian alphabets, Ogham and runes, and the high cross taken from Kilfenora in 1821. A Victorian glass and pitchpine screen now divides the aisleless nave from the crossing and the chancel, but one can see through it quite easily and the bare impressive interior is hardly affected. Fortunately the plaster has not been stripped from the walls and the interior is whitewashed which adds to the serenity of this lovely building. The transepts are now closed off from the body of the church. Along the walls of the choir between the thin lancets are corbels carrying the

The cross from Kilfenora

far left: **The lancets of the chancel seen from the crossing**

Details of voussoirs, capitals and jambs of the Romanesque doorway

The east front and tower reflected in the river Shannon

St Flannan's oratory

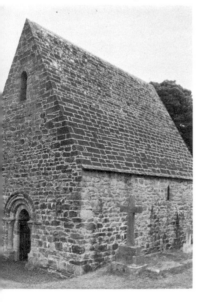

risers of the wooden roofs. These corbels have bellied capitals of foliage and one has a group of kilted gentlemen giving one another the kiss of peace – a gesture exactly suited to their surroundings. At the east end rise the three lights already mentioned, the two side ones pointed and the centre one with a round top. Their wide splays are held within an outer moulding richly carved in three orders rising to a pointed moulding with herringbone´ and lozenge carvings. Of all the many marvellous sights recorded in these pages there are few to compare with the perfect simplicity of these pencils of light. They are like angelic presences – and as difficult to photograph.

Outside the cathedral in the graveyard is the small Romanesque building called St Flannan's oratory, the nave of a church that has lost its chancel. Once it was thought to be much older than the twelfth century, but with its stone roof containing an upper chamber and its tunnel vault it now seems to be a work deriving from Cormac's chapel at Cashel.

Kilmacduagh

IT IS HARD TO IMAGINE an outline of hills more conducive to pleasurable contemplation than the rounded curves of the Burren Mountains. When to that outline the leaning round tower of Kilmacduagh, the grey ruined cathedral and its attendant churches and chapels are added in the foreground, then we are in the presence of a perfect marriage of architecture to a great landscape. A small reed-filled lough stretches to the west with the flat limestone beds rising gradually to the mountains. Up in the mountains was the oratory of that delightful saint, Colman Macduagh, who had a cockerel to call him to devotions, a mouse to nibble his ear if he fell asleep while praying or studying and a pet fly that would move along the page as he read to keep his place. One Easter day St Colman ended a year-long fast and

The round tower and cathedral with the Burren mountains beyond

Carving of a bishop

above right: **The chancel from the nave**

prayed for sustenance. At that very moment the silver dishes prepared in a banquet for King Guaire at his palace, five miles away, rose into the air and flew out of the windows of the royal hall. The king and his courtiers took to horse and rode after the flying banquet and came upon the saint surrounded by the dishes which had come to rest at his cell. Here the king gave the saint the lands at Kilmacduagh necessary for the founding of a monastery.

Besides the cathedral there are the substantial remains of three other churches: the twelfth-century St John the Baptist's church, St Mary's church of about 1200 and the church known as O'Heyne's, with remarkable carved capitals to the chancel arch which is early thirteenth-century. There also survive a fortified house (thirteenth-century and later) which was possibly the abbot's dwelling and the remains of another church. The round tower, which leans 15 inches out of true and is 120 feet high, retains its capped roof. It is, to my mind, the most beautiful round tower of all. What it is that makes these apparently simple structures so satisfying aesthetically is extremely difficult to analyse. Great height and the round form are two features, the one inspiring us, the other satisfying our instinctive desire for perfection. The gradual taper culminating in the cone of the capping, combining with the immense solidity of the masonry, signifies two aspects of true civilization: the union of strength with elegance. This tower is one of the earlier examples of its kind, and it stands near the ruined cathedral. The oldest part of the cathedral is the west wall (eleventh- or twelfth-century) which contains a blocked-up doorway with a flat lintel. The rest of the nave is about 1200 and the cathedral gained its present cruciform shape in the fifteenth century when the transepts were added. In the same period it acquired the finely moulded south door and some windows with attractive remaining tracery. In the north transept are naive carvings, two crucifixions and a bishop with an immense crozier moved to this transept from the south transept after 1765.

Limerick

ST MARY'S CATHEDRAL was founded by Domhnall Mor O'Brien, king of Thomond between 1180 and 1190. His tomb slab now lies at the foot of a great seventeenth-century tomb of a later O'Brien. The O'Briens continued to be closely associated with the cathedral and one of them, Donat O'Brien, bishop here in the early thirteenth century rebuilt the chancel and established the chapter of the cathedral. The original cathedral was very simple in plan, consisting of an aisleless chancel, transepts and aisled nave, reflecting in its severity the influence of the Cistercians who had arrived in Ireland four decades previously. A particularly impressive feature of the nave is the stern simplicity of the massive piers. The clerestory has round-topped windows over both the piers and the arches. Although most of this earlier building survives, it is masked, especially on the exterior, by the series of chapels constructed in the fourteenth and fifteenth centuries as extensions of the aisles by the rich merchant princes of Limerick. Several of these merchants are commemorated in surviving memorials such as the Galwey-Bultingfort tomb of about 1410. A later tomb is that of Cromwell's Irish ally, the O'Brien known for his destructiveness as Murrough of the Burnings. The rarest of the cathedral's furnishings, in Irish terms, is the set of misericords of about 1480, the only ones in the country, because of the ruin wrought by Murrough and his like, to survive.

below left: **The tower and exterior of the cathedral showing windows of different dates**

Details of the misericords: *above* **A lion fighting a wyvern** *and below* **an angel**

Scattery

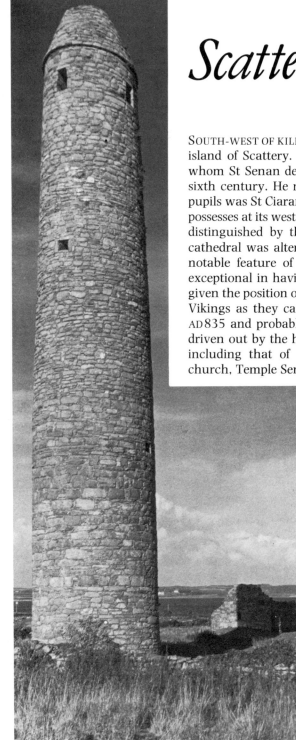

SOUTH-WEST OF KILRUSH in County Clare, in the mouth of the Shannon is the island of Scattery. The name comes from a dreadful monster called Cata whom St Senan defeated before founding his monastery here in the early sixth century. He made it an important centre of learning and one of his pupils was St Ciaran, the founder of Clonmacnois. The ruined cathedral still possesses at its west end antae and a lintelled doorway. These older parts, also distinguished by the use of large masonry, may be tenth century. The cathedral was altered in the thirteenth or fourteenth centuries. The most notable feature of the site is the round tower, 120 feet high, which is exceptional in having a doorway at ground level. It was probably unwise, given the position of the monastery which was the first prize available to the Vikings as they came up the Shannon. They plundered it in AD 816 and AD 835 and probably occupied it in the late tenth century until they were driven out by the high king, Brian Boru. There are other ruins on the site including that of three churches, a twelfth-century nave and chancel church, Temple Senan, and the fourteenth-century Church of the Dead.

The round
tower and
the cathedral

Tuam

TUAM WAS ONE OF THE FOUR archbishoprics of Ireland established in 1152. A cathedral was built here in County Galway on a site of a monastery founded by St Jarlath in the sixth century. Of this cathedral only the chancel with its arch remains. This red sandstone arch is, however, the grandest Irish Romanesque chancel arch in Ireland. With a huge span of almost 16 feet and with six orders of arch rising from five orders of pillars, it is a construction of exceptional technical skill; its voussoirs interlock so finely that there is no trace of deformation. On the four outer orders of the arch are variations of chevron and roll ornament, and an unusual spoonbill form is employed on the inner orders and the inside of the arch itself. One of the most charming features of this arch are the smiling, bearded faces engraved on the capitals of the half columns. Excellent carving, although very difficult to see, also remain on the splays of the chancel windows. At some unknown stage the nave westward of this arch was destroyed. Probably under Archbishop de Bermingham (1289–1312) the choir behind this chancel was built, buttressed and with the scheme of arched machicolation we have already seen at Kildare. The windows have interesting tracery which resemble some at Exeter Cathedral. The chancel arch became the west entrance to this cathedral and remained so, subject to the weather, until in 1861 Sir Thomas Deane was commissioned to build a new cathedral incorporating the Romanesque chancel as the east end of the choir. His large handsome church, which conveys an impression of greater antiquity than it could lay claim to because of the stalactites dripping from the capitals and the bloom of green mould on the blue-grey limestone, is marred by the extremely ugly stone furnishings of the choir which do much to detract from the great chancel arch.

below centre: **A face on a capital of the triumphal arch**

below left: **A detail showing the orders of the arch**

The triumphal arch of the chancel

Other medieval cathedrals

OF THE BRITISH ISLES

England and Wales

Only one English cathedral was totally lost on account of the Reformation: this was Coventry, a monastic cathedral co-equal with Lichfield. The medieval Coventry cathedral is not to be confused with the ruined shell that stands beside the modern cathedral. That was an important parish church raised to cathedral status in 1918 and destroyed by enemy action in 1940. Old St Paul's was lost in the Great Fire of London in 1666. It had a Norman nave, a central tower with a spire 520 feet high, thirteenth-century transepts, choir and Lady chapel with a notable rose window. The chapter house and cloisters, considered to be amongst the earliest examples of the Perpendicular style, were by William Ramsey (1332 onwards). Henry Yeveley also carried out works there, as did Inigo Jones who refaced the west portico. It was even longer than Winchester, 644 feet as compared to 554 feet. Only the splendour of its successor consoles us for its loss.

Several of the medieval collegiate churches and parish churches have been raised to cathedral status, such as Blackburn, Bradford, Brecon, Manchester, Newport, Bury St Edmunds and Wakefield. Westminster Abbey was a cathedral for only ten years, from 1540 to 1550.

Isle of Man

The ruins of the former cathedral of the bishops of Sodor and Man stand within the walls of a castle on St Patrick's island in Peel Bay harbour. Dedicated to St Germanus, it was under Norse and Scottish rule before the Isle was taken by the English in the fourteenth century. It remained, like Kirkwall, under the ecclesiastical jurisdiction of the Norwegian archbishop of Nidaros (Trondheim) until the fifteenth century.

Scotland

The earliest cathedral to be founded in these islands was the White House or *Candida Casa* built by St Ninian who began a community at Whithorn in Galloway in AD 397. Excavations have revealed a small church whose stones were coated in a light-coloured plaster and this is presumed to be St Ninian's original church. In about 1125 Whithorn became the church of the bishops of Galloway and later in the same century a priory of the Premonstratensian

Order was established there to serve the shrine. Of the priory church the thirteenth-century nave and a Romanesque doorway in the west front are among the chief remains. Of the other Scottish cathedrals there are Dornoch and Lismore. Dornoch was the cathedral of the bishops of Caithness and was begun in 1224. The cathedral was largely rebuilt in the 1830s by the Duchess of Sutherland. Important stonework, however, remains in the crossing, choir and parts of the transepts. Lismore was the cathedral of the bishops of Argyll until they removed to Iona in 1507. Situated on the island of Lismore in the mouth of the Linnhe Loch, the eighteenth-century parish church incorporates the chancel of the cathedral. Excavations have revealed traces of the nave and a west tower.

Ireland

It is the cathedrals of Ulster which have suffered most from destruction in war, neglect or over-restoration. The dioceses include Clogher, Enniskillen, Down and Connor, Dromore, Lisburn and Raphoe. The most important site is that of the primatial see of Armagh, founded by St Patrick in the fifth century. The cathedral begun by Archbishop O'Scanlan in 1261 was so completely altered in a series of restorations in the last century that two earlier authors writing on Irish cathedrals were driven to remark plaintively after recording these restorations: 'The reader might well ask if there are any remnants of veritable antiquity in a building so often defaced and burnt, and almost as frequently repaired and restored.' They point in answer to the crypt, the crossing piers, and reflect, carefully, that 'portions of successive restorations represent to a certain extent the older work'. St Columb's cathedral at Londonderry is interesting as an example of seventeenth-century Perpendicular, built between 1629 and 1633. This style was also employed in the rebuilding of St Carthage's cathedral at Lismore in County Waterford by the Earl of Cork in 1633. It incorporates some thirteenth-century work.

Other medieval cathedral churches included those at Killala, Achonry, Kilmore, Elphin, Ardagh, Emly and Ross. In many cases these sites are occupied by later buildings incorporating parts of earlier constructions. Those at Cork and Waterford wholly replace medieval churches. The cathedral at Leighlin contains some interesting fifteenth-century features, particularly in its window tracery. There are substantial remains of the priory church of Newtown Trim which also served as a cathedral.

Epilogue

SIR CHRISTOPHER WREN says in his *Memorials*, a miscellany of writings by himself and his son that, at the start of work on his new cathedral of St Paul's, when he and his chief mason had decided where the central point of the crossing should be, over which the dome was to rise, they sent a workman off to bring a stone from the rubble of the old cathedral to mark the spot. The workman chose a fragment at random and brought it to them. It had one word carved on it – *Resurgam* (I shall rise again).

Wren's great baroque cathedral was indeed a resurrection of a tradition and a scale of building for ecclesiastical architecture that had lapsed in England for over a hundred years since the Reformation. In that period terrible damage had been done to the medieval cathedrals especially under Edward VI and in the Cromwellian period. As can be seen from the preceding accounts, even worse devastation and neglect were visited upon the Scottish and Irish cathedrals. For all the losses to their glass, carvings and other furnishings, England and Wales were fortunate, at least, in that the Reformation Church of England retained the episcopacy and a liturgy that required the regular performance of choral music. This meant that the cathedrals were still necessary as the centres of administration for parishes and that they kept their chapters of deans and canons (or were provided with them where they had been monastic foundations). In Scotland the reform of the liturgy was far more extreme: the whole emphasis was on the Word and the necessity of hearing it. The cathedrals were too big and too awkward for this purpose and, where they were not allowed to fall into ruin, they were divided up to provide for several congregations as at Glasgow or St Giles, Edinburgh. The dioceses were secularized and placed under lay governors called Commendators. In Ireland the cathedrals were alienated from the mass of the population, partly because the new services were in English, a language as incomprehensible to most of them as the old Latin but without the merit of familiarity, and partly because the bishops were the appointees of the English government. For short periods during the various uprisings of the seventeenth century some of them were restored to the old liturgy, but after William of Orange's conquest of Ireland in 1691 they were firmly established in the possession of the Church of Ireland to which, where they are not in a ruinous state, they still belong. Despite the troubled conditions in Ireland in the seventeenth century, there was more cathedral building undertaken there than elsewhere in the British Isles; we have already noted Londonderry and Lismore, both built in a late Gothic style, and at Dromore the great devotional writer, Bishop Jeremy Taylor, rebuilt a cathedral which unfortunately no longer survives. In the eighteenth century new cathedrals

EDINBURGH: **a prospect of the choir**

were built at Cashel and Waterford. In England Wren's St Paul's was the only post-Reformation cathedral to be built until the nineteenth century. Then the rise in the population and the growth of new cities meant that the Church of England had to provide cathedrals for new dioceses, sometimes raising old abbey or collegiate churches to cathedral status, as, for example, St Albans or Ripon, or starting at Truro in 1880, building new ones. Catholic emancipation, followed by the restoration of the Roman Catholic hierarchy in Great Britain, gave an enormous impetus to cathedral building, the most notable being the neo-Byzantine Westminster Cathedral. In Scotland not only were several Roman Catholic cathedrals built, but also Scottish Episcopalian cathedrals such as William Butterfield's cathedral at Perth. In Ireland religious toleration enabled the rising Catholic middle class to donate large sums to the building of cathedrals that symbolized the triumph of their faith after the long years of suppression and persecution, in creations as diverse as the neo-classical pro-cathedral in Dublin and the neo-Gothic St Patrick's Roman Catholic cathedral at Armagh. The Church of Ireland too responded to the challenge of disestablishment in lavish buildings such as St Finbar's at Cork and St Anne's, Belfast. More cathedrals have followed in this century such as Guildford and Coventry, the latter because of enemy action that destroyed its predecessor. The most remarkable achievement in one city is that of Liverpool which now possesses two important cathedrals: one, Anglican, begun in 1904, built in traditional materials, the largest cathedral in the British Isles and still incomplete; the other, Roman Catholic, built 1962–67 of modern materials and in a modern idiom.

Of these post-Reformation cathedrals many are buildings of distinction and fulfil the functions for which they were designed as the regional centres of spiritual aspiration. Apart from Wren's St Paul's which is in a class on its own, they all suffer in comparison with the earlier cathedrals. This is because among the cathedrals of the Middle Ages are the greatest works of art ever made in these islands. Some, like Elgin, are only ruined and fragmentary skeletons of what they were; some, like Clonfert, are tiny and obscure; others such as Canterbury, Durham, Lincoln, and Wells survive, remarkably intact, much visited, used and loved. Whatever their state or scale, they give out a sense of life and work a magic upon us that almost always evaded the nineteenth-century and modern cathedral architects. They have had the advantages of technology, a much larger population as a pool to draw on for talent, the resources of scholarship for guidance and, in many cases, lavish funds – and in nearly every case the result has fallen short of the earlier achievements.

Where the medieval architects triumph over their later imitators is in their knowledge of how to make architecture, whether of interiors or exteriors, awaken our profoundest memories and emotions. Our great cathedrals unveil the greatness that is hidden in ourselves. Through the contemplation of shafted piers, traceried windows and suspended vaults, we are at home with sublimities of thought. In the calm of natural order revealed through intricacy of carving, in delight at contrasted textures of stone and light-filled glass, we recognize the extent of our own capacity for peace and joy. They have this effect on us, whatever our education, whatever our belief or lack of

CANTERBURY: **the nave and towers**

DURHAM: **the bishop's throne with beneath, under the traceried arch, the tomb of Bishop Hatfield**

WINCHESTER: **the west front**

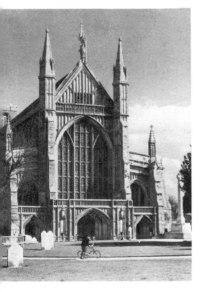

belief because, while we are in their presence or under their spell, they change our natures. This means that they are the product of an inspiration of a totally different order from the subjective and private inspiration of the modern artist. The link between artistic inspiration and mystical experience is an acknowledged fact for great numbers of medieval writers, artists and manuscript illuminators. The medieval architects were also trained draughtsmen, painters and sculptors, sharing a common attitude to art, its traditions and its sources. An artist can only express what he himself has experienced. The architects who made Durham, Kirkwall, some of the examples of Irish Romanesque and Transitional cathedrals and the great series of English and Scottish Gothic works must, therefore, have experienced in their own lives and natures the contemplative and mystical heights to which we respond in their buildings.

Art of this order has been called objective art. It can also be called the art of praise because, as the countless angels carved in the vaulting bosses or among the figure statues remind us, these cathedrals in their nature and function seek to perform on earth the continual service of praise which it is the nature of angels in heaven to provide. This ideal of art is implicit in the mystical works of Dionysius the Areopagite, first made available to the Christian West in the Dark Ages by the Irish scholar, John Scotus Eriugena, and which acted as an inspiration to patrons and artists of the Gothic period from Abbot Suger onwards. It was an ideal rediscovered by William Blake who was first inspired by Gothic art at the age of fifteen when clambering about the tombs of kings and queens in Westminster Abbey and drawing them for his first commission. Later he was to introduce the cathedral cities of England into his epic *Jerusalem* as spiritual beings. In our own century the nature of the art most supremely expressed in these cathedrals has been a source of fruitful speculation to scholars and philosophers such as Otto von Simson, Jacques Maritain, and P. D. Ouspensky who summed up what I have earlier been trying to express in this sentence: 'All true art is in fact nothing but an attempt to transmit the sensation of ecstasy.'

The part the cathedrals continue to play in our national life is shown by the responses of the public to the numerous appeals for the restoration and repair of their fabric. Immense efforts have continually to be made by deans and chapters, by ministers and elders, to maintain their edifices in a safe and functioning state. Theirs is no enviable task. The losses caused in restorations of the last century by recutting and replacing stonework have made many people very wary of what is legitimate replacement and what is unnecessary tampering. The argument still continues and has entered a different phase with the use of new chemicals on the statues of Wells and Exeter. There have been notable achievements, however, the draining of the soil beneath Winchester Cathedral by the diver, William Walker, and the recent work on the foundations of York Minster. Cleaning too has its supporters and detractors. There is also the question of the provision of new furnishings and works of art. Too many cathedrals and great churches have ugly and intrusive electric lighting installations and, what is almost worse, acoustical apparatus that completely destroys the intimate nature of regular cathedral services. What has happened to the lungs of our clerics that their voices need amplification to an extent which makes the most modest of preachers sound like a bombastic demagogue? And what has happened to our legs that we cannot stand or kneel during services but have to sit on chairs of plastic or plasticized wood whose textures debase their surroundings?

Those responsible for our cathedrals stand in a great tradition of men of all kinds and creeds who have allowed them to survive to the present day – the tradition of Archbishop Laud, Colonel Fiennes who defended William of Wykeham's tomb sword in hand against his own soldiers, Bishop Cosin who built the magnificent stalls and font cover at Durham after the Restoration, Dean Swift at Trinity, Dublin, John Shanks, a poor shoemaker who did all he could to preserve the ruins of Elgin in the early nineteenth century and the writers, critics and architects, Walter Scott, Pugin, Ruskin, William Morris among them, who did so much to educate public taste and to secure the preservation of our heritage. Such men are well fitted to Isaiah's words (Isaiah 58, 12), 'thou shalt raise up the foundations of many generations; and thou shalt be called, The repairer of the breach, The restorer of paths to dwell in.'

WELLS: **view from the moat of the Bishop's palace**

Glossary

Aisles: the walks parallel to the nave or central portion of a church

Ambulatory: the walk round an apse or polygonal eastern end

Antae: projections of the side walls beyond the gables, a feature of many early Irish churches

Apse: semi-circular or polygonal eastern termination

Arcade: a range of arches supported on piers or columns. Blind arcade means a range of arches in a wall

Arch: a structure of radiating blocks (voussoirs) over an opening held together by lateral pressure

Ballflower: decoration popular in the early fourteenth century consisting of a three-petalled flower enclosing a ball

Basilica: originally a term for Roman law courts and then applied to large Christian churches as at Rome; the origin of the nave-and-aisles plan

Battlement: a castellated parapet

Bay: the structural subdivision of a building, e.g. the compartments into which a nave or vaulted roof is divided

Buttress: a strengthening mass of masonry projected from a wall, usually at a point of concentrated load, to provide extra stability

Canopy: the hood over a niche, altar or stall

Capital: a block, usually decorated, between the shafts of a pier, or a column, and the load above

Censer: a vessel in which incense is burnt, hence 'censing', the action of swinging a censer

Centering: the wooden framework on which an arch or vault is constructed

Chancel: a general term for the eastern part of a church containing the high altar, meaning the part divided from the rest by a screen

Chantry chapel: a chapel endowed for saying mass for the donor, who was frequently buried in it

Chevet: the French term for the eastern end of a church, generally polygonal

Chevron: a term used for Norman zigzag moulding

Choir: the part of the church where the service is sung, a term often loosely applied to the eastern part of a church

Cinquefoil: *see* foil

Clerestory: the upper stage with windows in a church that rises above adjacent roofs

Corbel: a projecting block of stone, often carved or moulded, supporting a load above

Crocket: a projecting stone ornamentation carved like foliage, decorating the angles of spires or canopies

Crossing: the space where the nave, transepts and chancel intersect

Crypt: the room usually underground below the chancel

Cushion capital: a capital cut from a square block and rounded at the base

Dogtooth: a favourite Early English form of ornamentation, resembling a row of teeth

Easter sepulchre: a tomb chest set in a recess on which an effigy of Christ or the sacrament was laid in Easter services

Finial: the top part of a pinnacle or canopy

Flamboyant: the name for the late French Gothic style, called after the flame-like tracery which distinguishes it

Foil: the leaf-shape formed by the cusping of Gothic tracery, as in trefoil (three-lobed), quatrefoil (four-lobed), etc.

Gable: the triangle at the top of a wall formed by the sloping lines of the roof

Galilee: a projecting porch also used as a chapel (*see* Durham, Ely and Lincoln)

Gallery: the upper storey over an aisle with arches opening on the nave, also called the tribune

Gargoyle: a grotesquely carved projecting waterspout

Garth: a garden or lawn enclosed by a cloister

Hall church: a church in which the nave and aisles are of the same height

Hood-mould: the moulding projecting over arches of doorways and windows to throw off rain

Jambs: the upright sides of doors and windows

Lancet: a narrow pointed window, a feature of the Early English style

Lantern: the part of a central tower rising above the roofs and lit with windows

Lierne: *see* vault

Lintel: the horizontal beam or stone across an opening

Machicolation: a parapet projecting on corbels with open spaces between them for dropping missiles

Misericord: a hinged seat, carved on the underside, to give support to someone standing during a service

Moulding: the contours given to projecting members, as in the carving of an arch

Mullion: the upright posts that divide a window into lights

Ogee: *see* arch

Order (of a doorway or window): the bands of moulding or carving receding inwards

Parapet: the part of the wall rising above the roof gutter

Pendant: a long boss hanging from a ceiling or roof

Pier: a shaped length of wall, generally used here for the mass of masonry from which an arch springs in an arcade

Pinnacle: a turret-like termination on buttresses and parapets

Presbytery: the space for the clergy at the east end of a church, often used as a synonym for sanctuary

Pulpitum: the stone screen at the entrance to the choir

Quatrefoil: *see* foil

Reredos: the screen rising behind the high altar

Retable: an altarpiece

Retrochoir: the parts of a church behind the high altar

Rib-vault: *see* vault

Rood: a crucifix, hence 'rood-screen', the screen on which a crucifix is erected

Rose window: also called a wheel window; a round window whose mullions converge like the spokes of a wheel

Sanctuary: the space round the high altar

Sedilia: seats for priests on the south side of the sanctuary

Shaft: a thin column often forming part of a clustered pier or rising from the pier or from a corbel to support a rib of the vaulting

Spandrel: the space between the apices of two arches

Spire: the tall cone or pyramid set on a tower

Stalls: carved seats in wood or stone set in a row

Stiff-leaf: stylized carved foliage of the Early English style

Strainer arch: an arch inserted to give support as in the crossing at Wells

Tabernacle: an elaborately carved niche or canopy

Thrust: lateral force exerted, e.g., by arches or sloping roofs, often resisted by buttresses

Tierceron: *see* vault

Tracery: ornamental stonework in patterns in the upper parts of Gothic windows or the raised decoration on wall surfaces

Transom: the horizontal or cross-divisions of a window

Transepts: the lateral divisions, projecting north and south, generally from the crossing of a church but also applied to similar projections from the choir and west end

Tribune: *see* gallery

Triforium: the arcaded wall passage or blind arcading below the clerestory windows

Tympanum: the space enclosed between the lintel of a doorway (or arcading) and the arch

Vault: arched covering in stone, exhibiting many variations in our period, from the tunnel or barrel vault to the groined vault in the Norman period consisting of two tunnel vaults intersecting at right angles. The groined vault when given projecting ribs along the groins makes the rib-vault. The ridge rib, introduced in the early thirteenth century, is a rib running longitudinally along a vault or, transversely, across it. A tierceron rib is a secondary rib issuing from a main springing and joining the longitudinal ridge rib. A lierne rib is one that does not issue either from a main springer or from a central boss. Fan vaulting, a late medieval invention, has all its ribs of equal radii and similar curvature

Voussoirs: the wedge-shaped blocks of which an arch is formed

Short bibliography

THERE ARE ACCOUNTS of all the English cathedrals in the now completed volumes of *The Buildings of England* (Penguin Books) edited by Sir Nikolaus Pevsner. The Bell series of books on the English and Welsh cathedrals issued from the 1890s onwards is still of great value. Nearly every cathedral issues its own guidebook and these vary considerably in depth of treatment. There are also HMSO guides to some of the Scottish cathedrals and sites. Among the books consulted for the writing of this volume and which may be useful for further reading are:

ALEC CLIFTON-TAYLOR: *The cathedrals of England*. London, 1967

BRIAN DE BREFFNY & G. MOTT: *The churches and abbeys of Ireland*. London, 1977

ELEANOR DUCKETT: *The wandering saints*. London, 1959

PAUL FRANKL: *The Gothic: literary sources and interpretations through eight centuries*. Princeton, 1960

JOHN FITCHIN: *The construction of Gothic cathedrals*. Oxford, 1961

IAN C. HANNAH: *The story of Scotland in stone*. Edinburgh & London, 1934

PETER HARBISON: *Guide to the national monuments in the Republic of Ireland*. Dublin, 1975

JOHN HARVEY: *Cathedrals of England and Wales*. Revised edn. London, 1974

H. R. LEASK: *Irish churches and monastic buildings*. 3 vols. Dundalk, 1955–60

DAVID MACGIBBON & THOMAS ROSS: *Ecclesiastical architecture of Scotland to the seventeenth century*. 3 vols. Edinburgh, 1896–97

W. DOUGLAS SIMPSON: *The ancient stones of Scotland*. London, 1969

Index

DATE DUE		
JUN 7 1989		
MAY 18 1990		
OCT 12 '92		
Dec. 03 98		
NOV 1 1 2001